W9-DFQ-707

stir-fry

HOMESTYLE

stir-fry

MURDOCH BOOKS

contents

Speedy stir-frying 6

Beef 8

Pork 40

Lamb 78

Chicken and duck 94

Seafood 148

Tofu and tempeh 198

Vegetables 218

Basics—curry pastes and more 244

Index 250

Speedy stir-frying

The art of stir-frying was, like many clever culinary inventions, born of utter necessity. Although the ancient Chinese ruling classes enjoyed lives of plenty and pleasure, their minions did not. Indeed, fuel and oil for cooking—and even water—were all in short supply. How did one cook under such conditions? Quickly, it would seem—to make the most of that precious fuel. What was needed was a cooking vessel that provided a large surface area (for the utmost cooking efficiency) and had the ability to heat swiftly ... enter the wok. That was some 2000 years ago and the rest, as they say, is history.

Many foods and various ingredient combinations are suited to stir-frying. The only requirements are: that the ingredients are tender, they are firstly cut into small pieces and the heat used is fairly fierce. Seafood, tofu, beef, lamb, pork and chicken are all perfect candidates, as are many vegetables, noodles and even nuts. These—often in combination with aromatic touches such as ginger, garlic, lemongrass, curry pastes and lush herbs—make for meals that are a taste and texture sensation, needing little in the way of accompaniments except, of course, for piles of fluffy steamed rice. From Mongolian lamb stir-fry to Goan-style chicken with sultanas and almonds; Vietnamese chicken with pineapple and cashews and Balinese chilli squid, the recipes here are a luscious *tour de force* of the fascinating cuisines of Asia. Some stir-fries are suited to everyday, family-type dinners (Nasi goreng; curried sweet potato stir-fry; and sesame pork, for example) while others are worthy of special occasions, when there's more time and money to spend. Consider duck, orange and bok-choy; chicken with walnuts and straw mushrooms; or prawns and scallops with Thai spices for your next dinner party. Sure there's a bit of preparation, but once all the peeling, pounding and chopping is done, all that's left is to fire up the wok and the cooking's done in a flash—with a few dramatic tosses and a hiss and a roar.

Beef

Warm citrus beef salad

PREPARATION TIME: 25 MINUTES I TOTAL COOKING TIME: 15 MINUTES I SERVES 4

oil, for cooking
500 g (1 lb 2 oz) rump or sirloin steak,
    thinly sliced
1 onion, sliced
2 garlic cloves, crushed
1 teaspoon grated fresh ginger
1 teaspoon grated lemon zest (see HINT)
1 teaspoon grated orange zest
1 tablespoon lemon juice
1 tablespoon orange juice
100 g (3½ oz) rocket (arugula) leaves
40 g (1½ oz) snow pea (mangetout) sprouts
1 lemon, segmented
1 orange, segmented

NUTRITION PER SERVE
Protein 30 g; Fat 15 g; Carbohydrate 7 g; Dietary
Fibre 3 g; Cholesterol 85 mg; 1145 kJ (275 Cal)

1 Heat the wok until very hot, add 1 tablespoon of the oil and swirl it around to coat the side. Stir-fry the beef in batches until well browned, adding more oil when necessary. Remove all the beef from the wok and set aside.

2 Reheat the wok, add 1 tablespoon of the oil and stir-fry the onion, garlic and ginger for 3–4 minutes, or until the onion is tender. Return the meat to the wok along with the combined lemon and orange zest and juice.

3 Bring to the boil, then toss the rocket through the beef mixture and cook until the rocket is just wilted. Serve immediately on a bed of snow pea sprouts, surrounded by the lemon and orange segments.

HINT: *Grate the zest you need from the lemon and orange, before peeling and segmenting them to add to the stir-fry. Collect the juice in a bowl as you segment them.*

To segment the orange, cut a slice off the top and bottom in order to stabilise it.

Remove the zest and pith, following the curve of the orange.

Cut out the segments by slicing between the membrane and flesh on each side.

Marinated lemongrass beef

PREPARATION TIME: 15 MINUTES + 3–4 HOURS MARINATING | TOTAL COOKING TIME: 15 MINUTES | SERVES 4

500 g (1 lb 2 oz) rump steak, thinly sliced
3 lemongrass stems, white part only,
    finely chopped
1 onion, finely chopped
3 garlic cloves, finely chopped
2 tablespoons fish sauce
2 teaspoons sugar
1 tablespoon oil
40 g (1½ oz/¼ cup) chopped roasted peanuts
coriander (cilantro) leaves, to serve

1   Put the steak in a large glass or ceramic bowl.
Mix the lemongrass, onion, garlic, fish sauce,
sugar and oil to make a marinade. Pour over the
meat and toss well. Cover and refrigerate for
3–4 hours.

2   Heat the wok until very hot and stir-fry the
beef in two batches over high heat until it is just
browned. Toss constantly to make sure the small
pieces of onion and lemongrass don't catch on
the wok and burn.

3   Return all the meat to the wok. Add the
roasted peanuts and toss quickly until combined.
Serve immediately on a bed of coriander leaves.

NUTRITION PER SERVE
Protein 35 g; Fat 8.5 g; Carbohydrate 6 g; Dietary
Fibre 2 g; Cholesterol 85 mg; 980 kJ (235 Cal)

Using a large sharp knife, cut the rump steak into
thin strips.

Finely chop the lemongrass using only the white
part of the stems.

Combine the lemongrass, onion, garlic, fish sauce,
sugar and oil with the meat.

Black bean beef with noodles

PREPARATION TIME: 15 MINUTES | TOTAL COOKING TIME: 10 MINUTES | SERVES 4

250 g (9 oz) instant noodles
500 g (1 lb 2 oz) beef, thinly sliced
2 teaspoons sesame oil
2 garlic cloves, crushed
1 tablespoon grated fresh ginger
oil, for cooking
6 spring onions (scallions), sliced on
    the diagonal
1 small red capsicum (pepper), thinly sliced
125 g (4½ oz) snow peas (mangetouts), halved
    on the diagonal
4 tablespoons black bean and garlic sauce
    (see HINT)
2 tablespoons hoisin sauce
60 g (2¼ oz/⅔ cup) bean sprouts

1   Cook the noodles according to the manufacturer's directions, then drain and keep warm.

2   Place the beef, sesame oil, garlic and ginger in a bowl and mix together well. Heat the wok until very hot, add 1 tablespoon of the oil and swirl it around to coat the side. Add half the beef and stir-fry for 2–3 minutes, or until the beef is just cooked. Remove from the wok, add a little more of the oil and cook the rest of the beef. Remove all the beef from the wok.

3   Heat 1 tablespoon of the oil in the wok. Add the spring onion, capsicum and snow peas and stir-fry for 2 minutes. Return the beef to the wok and stir in the black bean and garlic sauce, hoisin sauce and 1 tablespoon water.

4   Add the noodles to the wok and toss to heat through. Serve immediately, topped with bean sprouts.

HINT: *Black bean and garlic sauce is available at Asian grocery stores or good supermarkets.*

NUTRITION PER SERVE
Protein 30 g; Fat 20 g; Carbohydrate 25 g; Dietary Fibre 5.7 g; Cholesterol 76 mg; 1751 kJ (418 Cal)

Add the beef and marinade to the wok and stir-fry in two batches over high heat.

Stir-fry the spring onion, capsicum and snow peas for 2 minutes.

Quick beef and noodle salad

PREPARATION TIME: 15 MINUTES | TOTAL COOKING TIME: 10 MINUTES | SERVES 4

500 g (1 lb 2 oz) rump steak
1 tablespoon peanut oil
2 tablespoons oyster sauce
2 teaspoons mild curry powder
1 tablespoon soft brown sugar
1 small Lebanese (short) cucumber,
    thinly sliced
1 red onion, sliced
1 red capsicum (pepper), thinly sliced
1 small red chilli, seeded and chopped
1 very large handful chopped mint
60 g (2¼ oz/⅓ cup) chopped unsalted
    peanuts or cashews
500 g (1 lb 2 oz) hokkien (egg) noodles

DRESSING
125 ml (4 fl oz/½ cup) rice vinegar
    (see HINT)
2 tablespoons fish sauce
60 g (2¼ oz/¼ cup) caster (superfine) sugar
2 teaspoons finely chopped fresh ginger
1 small red chilli, seeded and chopped
1 tablespoon chopped coriander
    (cilantro) leaves

1   Remove all visible fat from the meat. Combine the peanut oil, oyster sauce, curry powder and brown sugar in a small bowl.

2   Heat a wok over medium heat. Add the steak and cook for 6–8 minutes, turning and basting with half the sauce during cooking. Remove the steak from the wok.

3   To make the dressing, whisk together all the ingredients.

4   Place the cucumber, onion, capsicum and chilli in a large bowl. Add the mint and nuts. Thinly slice the meat, add to the bowl with the dressing and lightly toss to combine. If you have time, leave for a few minutes to marinate.

5   Place the noodles in the same wok and stir-fry over medium heat for 1–2 minutes. Stir in the remaining basting sauce and toss until heated through. Divide the noodles among serving bowls and top with the salad. Serve immediately.

HINT: *Rice vinegar is available in Asian grocery stores.*

NUTRITION PER SERVE
Protein 50 g; Fat 17 g; Carbohydrate 115 g; Dietary Fibre 5.5 g; Cholesterol 105 mg; 3405 kJ (815 Cal)

While you cook the steak, turn it and baste often with the sauce.

Place the cucumber, onion, capsicum and chilli in a large bowl and add the mint and nuts.

Stir the remaining basting sauce into the noodles in the wok.

Beef with oyster sauce

PREPARATION TIME: 15 MINUTES | TOTAL COOKING TIME: 5 MINUTES | SERVES 4

1½ teaspoons cornflour (cornstarch)
125 ml (4 fl oz/½ cup) beef stock
2 tablespoons oyster sauce
1 teaspoon finely crushed garlic
1 teaspoon caster (superfine) sugar
oil, for cooking
350 g (12 oz) rump steak, thinly sliced
250 g (9 oz) beans, topped and tailed, cut into
    5 cm (2 inch) lengths
1 small red capsicum (pepper), sliced
60 g (2¼ oz/⅔ cup) bean sprouts

1 Dissolve the cornflour in a little of the stock. Mix with the remaining stock, oyster sauce, garlic and sugar and set aside.

2 Heat the wok until very hot, add 1 tablespoon of the oil and swirl it around to coat the side. Add the beef in batches and stir-fry over high heat for 2 minutes, or until it browns.

3 Return all the beef to the wok. Add the beans and capsicum and stir-fry for another minute.

4 Add the cornflour mixture to the wok and cook until the sauce boils and thickens. Stir in the bean sprouts and serve immediately.

NUTRITION PER SERVE
Protein 23 g; Fat 12 g; Carbohydrate 10 g; Dietary Fibre 2.5 g; Cholesterol 60 mg; 1016 kJ (243 Cal)

Brown the steak in batches so the wok doesn't overcrowd and reduce the temperature.

Add the beans and capsicum to the browned meat and stir-fry for 1 minute.

Add the mixture of stock and cornflour and stir until the sauce boils and thickens.

Chinese beef and snow peas

PREPARATION TIME: 10 MINUTES I TOTAL COOKING TIME: 5 MINUTES I SERVES 4

400 g (14 oz) rump steak, thinly sliced
2 tablespoons soy sauce
½ teaspoon grated fresh ginger
oil, for cooking
200 g (7 oz) snow peas (mangetouts), trimmed
1½ teaspoons cornflour (cornstarch)
125 ml (4 fl oz/½ cup) beef stock
1 teaspoon soy sauce, extra
¼ teaspoon sesame oil

1 Put the meat in a glass or ceramic bowl. Mix the soy sauce and ginger and add to the meat. Stir well. Heat the wok until very hot, add 2 tablespoons of the oil and swirl it around to coat the side. Add the beef and snow peas and stir-fry over high heat for 2 minutes, or until the meat changes colour.

2 Dissolve the cornflour in a little of the stock. Add to the wok with the remaining stock, extra soy and sesame oil.

3 Stir until the sauce boils and thickens. Serve immediately.

HINT: *To make the beef easier to slice, freeze it until it is just firm and slice while it is still frozen.*

NUTRITION PER SERVE
Protein 27 g; Fat 13 g; Carbohydrate 9 g; Dietary Fibre 3 g; Cholesterol 67 mg; 1088 kJ (260 Cal)

Stir-fry the beef and snow peas over high heat until the meat browns.

Dissolve the cornflour in a little of the stock and add to the wok with the rest of the stock.

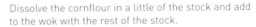

Stir the beef and snow peas until the sauce comes to the boil and thickens.

Mee goreng

PREPARATION TIME: 45 MINUTES | TOTAL COOKING TIME: 10 MINUTES | SERVES 4

1 large onion, finely chopped
2 garlic cloves, finely chopped
2 red chillies, seeded and finely chopped
2 cm (¾ inch) piece fresh ginger, grated
oil, for cooking
350 g (12 oz) hokkien (egg) noodles, gently
  pulled apart (see HINT)
500 g (1 lb 2 oz) peeled raw
  prawns (shrimp)
250 g (9 oz) rump steak, thinly sliced
4 spring onions (scallions), chopped
1 large carrot, cut into matchsticks
2 celery stalks, cut into matchsticks
1 tablespoon kecap manis (see NOTE)
1 tablespoon soy sauce
1 tablespoon tomato sauce (ketchup)

NUTRITION PER SERVE
Protein 43 g; Fat 17 g; Carbohydrate 14 g; Dietary
Fibre 2.5 g; Cholesterol 230 mg; 1600 kJ (380 Cal)

1 Combine the onion, garlic, chilli and ginger in a small food processor or mortar and pestle. Process in short bursts, or pound, until a paste forms, adding a little oil to help the grinding, if necessary.

2 Heat the wok until very hot, add 1 tablespoon of the oil and swirl it around to coat the side. Stir-fry the noodles until plump and warmed through. Transfer to a serving plate; cover to keep warm.

3 Add another tablespoon of oil to the wok and stir-fry the paste until golden. Add the prawns, steak, spring onion, carrot and celery and stir-fry for 2–3 minutes. Add the kecap manis, soy and tomato sauces and season well with salt and pepper. Serve immediately over the noodles.

HINT: *Hokkien noodles are thick yellow noodles that have already been cooked and are ready to use. If they are not available, you can use dried egg noodles, but they must be cooked and drained well beforehand.*

NOTE: *Kecap manis is a thick, sweet soy sauce. If you cannot find it, use regular soy sauce mixed with a little soft brown sugar.*

Gently prise apart the hokkien noodles before heating in the wok.

Stir-fry the noodles in the wok until they are warmed through.

Heat the oil in the wok and stir-fry the paste mixture until it is golden.

Thai beef salad

PREPARATION TIME: 20 MINUTES + COOLING I TOTAL COOKING TIME: 5 MINUTES I SERVES 6

oil, for cooking
500 g (1 lb 2 oz) beef fillet or lean rump steak, thinly sliced
2 garlic cloves, crushed
1 very large handful coriander (cilantro) roots and stems, finely chopped
1 tablespoon grated palm sugar (jaggery)
80 ml (2½ fl oz/⅓ cup) lime juice
2 tablespoons fish sauce
¼ teaspoon ground white pepper
2 small red chillies, seeded and thinly sliced
2 red Asian shallots (eschalots), thinly sliced
2 telegraph (long) cucumbers, sliced into thin ribbons
2 very large handfuls mint leaves
90 g (3¼ oz/1 cup) bean sprouts
30 g (1 oz/¼ cup) chopped roasted peanuts

1 Heat the wok until very hot, add 1 tablespoon of the oil and swirl it around to coat the side. Add half the beef and cook for 1–2 minutes, or until medium-rare. Remove from the wok and set aside. Repeat with the rest of the beef.

2 Place the garlic, coriander, palm sugar, lime juice, fish sauce, white pepper and ¼ teaspoon salt in a bowl, and stir until all the sugar has dissolved. Add the chilli and shallots and mix well.

3 Pour the sauce over the beef while still hot, mix well, then cool to room temperature.

4 In a separate bowl, toss together the cucumber and mint leaves, and refrigerate until required.

5 Place the cucumber and mint on a serving platter, and top with the beef, bean sprouts and roasted peanuts. Serve immediately.

Wear disposable rubber gloves while preparing hot chillies. Remove the seeds and thinly slice.

Pour the sauce over the hot stir-fried beef and leave to cool.

NUTRITION PER SERVE
Protein 22 g; Fat 13 g; Carbohydrate 7.5 g; Dietary Fibre 2 g; Cholesterol 50 mg; 1041 kJ (248 Cal)

Beef with shiitake mushrooms

PREPARATION TIME: 25 MINUTES + 10 MINUTES SOAKING | TOTAL COOKING TIME: 15 MINUTES | SERVES 4

6 dried shiitake mushrooms
400 g (14 oz) topside steak, thinly sliced
oil, for cooking
4 garlic cloves, finely chopped
1 red chilli, finely chopped
2 onions, very thinly sliced
4 spring onions (scallions), chopped
½ red capsicum (pepper), thinly sliced
125 ml (4 fl oz/½ cup) tomato passata
   (puréed tomatoes)
2 teaspoons soft brown sugar
2 tomatoes, diced
2 teaspoons sesame oil
2 tablespoons shredded basil leaves

1   Put the dried shiitake mushrooms in a bowl and cover with boiling water. Leave to soak for 10 minutes, or until they have plumped up. Drain and thinly slice.

2   Put the steak in a bowl. Mix together 2 tablespoons of the oil, the garlic, chilli and some salt and pepper and add to the steak. Toss well.

3   Heat the wok until very hot and stir-fry the steak in two batches over high heat for 30 seconds, or until just browned. Reheat the wok in between each batch. Remove steak from the wok.

4   Reheat the wok, add 2 tablespoons of the oil and stir-fry the onion, spring onion and capsicum for 3 minutes, or until golden. Add the mushrooms, tomato passata and sugar. Bring to the boil, then reduce the heat and simmer for 3 minutes. Add the beef, tomato and sesame oil, and season. Bring to the boil, allowing the tomato to heat through. Stir in the basil. Serve immediately.

NUTRITION PER SERVE
Protein 25 g; Fat 15 g; Carbohydrate 8 g; Dietary Fibre 3 g; Cholesterol 50 mg; 1125 kJ (270 Cal)

Soak the dried shiitake mushrooms in boiling water until they plump up.

Add the chopped mushrooms and tomato passata to the onion mix.

Mandarin beef

PREPARATION TIME: 25 MINUTES + 15 MINUTES MARINATING | TOTAL COOKING TIME: 5 MINUTES | SERVES 4

350 g (12 oz) boned rib eye steak,
    thinly sliced
2 teaspoons soy sauce
2 teaspoons dry sherry
1 teaspoon chopped fresh ginger
1 teaspoon sesame oil
oil, for cooking
¼ teaspoon ground white pepper
2 teaspoons finely chopped dried mandarin
    or tangerine zest, plus extra to garnish
2 teaspoons soy sauce, extra
1½ teaspoons caster (superfine) sugar
1½ teaspoons cornflour (cornstarch)
4 tablespoons beef stock

1 Place the meat in a bowl. Mix the soy sauce, sherry, ginger and sesame oil together, add to the meat and toss well. Leave to marinate for 15 minutes.

2 Heat the wok until very hot, add 1 tablespoon of the oil and swirl it around to coat the side. Add the beef and stir-fry over high heat for 2 minutes, or until the meat is browned on all sides.

3 Add the pepper, dried mandarin or tangerine zest, extra soy sauce and sugar. Stir-fry briefly.

4 Dissolve the cornflour in a little of the stock and then add the remaining stock. Pour the whole lot into the wok. Stir until the sauce boils and thickens. Serve immediately garnished with extra zest.

VARIATION: *For a hotter dish, fry a whole dried chilli in the hot oil and then discard the chilli before adding the beef to the wok.*

HINT: *The more expensive, tender cuts of beef such as rib eye or rump are best for stir-frying. However, a cheaper cut such as round or blade can be used, but should be tenderised in a marinade after it has been thinly sliced. Dissolve ½ teaspoon bicarbonate of soda (baking soda) in 2 tablespoons warm water. Place beef in a dish, pour over soda mixture and knead it through meat. Cover and refrigerate for 2 hours. Bring to room temperature, then continue with recipe.*

NUTRITION PER SERVE
Protein 20 g; Fat 8 g; Carbohydrate 9 g; Dietary Fibre 0 g; Cholesterol 60 mg; 785 kJ (188 Cal)

Make a marinade from the soy sauce, sherry, ginger and sesame oil and toss through the meat.

Add the pepper, zest, soy sauce and sugar to the browned meat and stir-fry for 1 minute.

Add the mixture of stock and cornflour and stir until the sauce boils and thickens.

Beef with spinach

PREPARATION TIME: 20 MINUTES + 2 HOURS MARINATING | TOTAL COOKING TIME: 15 MINUTES | SERVES 4

500 g (1 lb 2 oz) rump or sirloin steak, thinly sliced
60 ml (2 fl oz/¼ cup) sweet chilli sauce
2 tablespoons soy sauce
1 garlic clove, crushed
2 teaspoons grated fresh ginger
1 tablespoon sherry
oil, for cooking
2 onions, cut into wedges
500 g (1 lb 2 oz/1 bunch) English spinach leaves, shredded

1   Combine the steak with the sweet chilli sauce, soy sauce, garlic, ginger and sherry. Cover and refrigerate for at least 2 hours, or overnight.

2   Drain the meat, discarding the marinade. Heat the wok until very hot, add 1 tablespoon of the oil and swirl it around to coat the side. Stir-fry the meat in batches over high heat until it is well browned, adding more oil when necessary. Remove from the wok and set aside.

3   Reheat the wok, add 1 tablespoon of the oil and stir-fry the onion wedges for 3–4 minutes, or until tender. Return the meat to the wok.

4   Just before serving, toss the English spinach through the beef mixture until the spinach is just wilted. Serve immediately.

Carefully slice the rump or sirloin steak into thin strips across the grain.

Drain all the liquid from the marinated meat, using a sieve.

NUTRITION PER SERVE
Protein 35 g; Fat 15 g; Carbohydrate 6.5 g; Dietary Fibre 5 g; Cholesterol 85 mg; 1200 kJ (285 Cal)

Coriander beef

PREPARATION TIME: 15 MINUTES + 1–2 HOURS MARINATING | TOTAL COOKING TIME: 15 MINUTES | SERVES 4

500 g (1 lb 2 oz) rump steak, thinly sliced
4 garlic cloves, finely chopped
1 tablespoon finely chopped fresh ginger
1 very large handful coriander (cilantro) roots,
    stems and leaves, chopped
60 ml (2 fl oz/¼ cup) oil, plus extra
    for cooking
2 red onions, thinly sliced
½ red capsicum (pepper), thinly sliced
½ green capsicum (pepper), thinly sliced
1 tablespoon lime juice
1 very large handful coriander (cilantro)
    leaves, chopped, extra

1 Place the beef strips in a glass or ceramic bowl. Add the garlic, ginger, coriander and oil. Mix together well, then cover and refrigerate for 1–2 hours.

2 Heat the wok until very hot and stir-fry the meat with its marinade in three batches over high heat for 2–3 minutes, or until the meat is just cooked. Remove all the meat from the wok and keep it warm.

3 Heat 1 tablespoon oil, add the onion and cook over medium-high heat for 3–4 minutes, or until the onion is slightly softened. Add the capsicum and cook, tossing constantly, for 3–4 minutes, or until the capsicum is slightly softened.

4 Return all the meat to the wok with the lime juice and extra coriander. Toss well, then remove from the heat and season well with salt and cracked black pepper. Serve immediately.

NUTRITION PER SERVE
Protein 30 g; Fat 25 g; Carbohydrate 5 g; Dietary Fibre 2 g; Cholesterol 85 mg; 1620 kJ (385 Cal)

Using a sharp knife, finely chop the roots, stems and leaves of the coriander.

Stir-fry the marinated meat in batches until it is just cooked.

Chilli beef with Chinese spinach

PREPARATION TIME: 30 MINUTES + 20 MINUTES MARINATING | TOTAL COOKING TIME: 15 MINUTES | SERVES 3–4

500 g (1 lb 2 oz) rump or fillet steak

2 tablespoons rice wine

1 tablespoon cornflour (cornstarch)

4 tablespoons soy sauce

3 tablespoons peanut oil

250 g (9 oz) baby Chinese spinach with
    pink roots

2 tablespoons canned salted black beans

2 teaspoons finely chopped fresh ginger

2 garlic cloves, finely chopped

1 long green chilli, seeded and thinly sliced

1 long red chilli, seeded and thinly sliced

1 tablespoon sesame oil

1 teaspoon sugar

2 teaspoons peanut oil, extra

4 garlic cloves, extra, thinly sliced

1 Trim the meat of any excess fat and sinew and slice across the grain into thin strips. Combine the rice wine, cornflour and 2 tablespoons of the soy sauce in a bowl. Stir in 1 tablespoon of the peanut oil. Add the beef and mix well to coat. Cover and leave to marinate in the refrigerator for 20 minutes.

2 Wash and dry the spinach. Leave the pink roots on, but trim away the straggly ends. Cut the leaves from the stems, as these will need less cooking. Rinse the black beans under cold running water, then drain and mash.

3 Drain the meat and discard the marinade. Heat 1 tablespoon of the peanut oil in a wok and cook the meat quickly over high heat, in two batches, until just browned. Do not overcook. Remove from the wok and set aside.

4 Heat the remaining peanut oil in the wok and stir-fry the ginger, garlic, chilli and black beans for 1–2 minutes. Return the beef to the wok with the sesame oil, sugar and remaining soy sauce. Stir-fry briefly until the beef is heated through. Remove from the wok, cover and set aside. Keep warm.

5 Working quickly, wipe out the wok with paper towels and heat the extra peanut oil. Add the sliced garlic and cook for about 30 seconds, until it is lightly golden. Add the spinach stems and 1 tablespoon water. Stir-fry for 30 seconds, until the stems are bright green. Add the spinach leaves and toss until just wilted. Serve immediately with the beef.

NUTRITION PER SERVE (4)
Protein 35 g; Fat 25 g; Carbohydrate 5 g; Dietary
Fibre 3 g; Cholesterol 85 mg; 1615 kJ (385 Cal)

Use a glass or ceramic bowl when marinating in an acid mixture that contains wine or citrus juice.

Stir-fry the beef in batches so that the wok doesn't overcrowd and the meat fries rather than stews.

Add the spinach leaves to the wok and toss until they have wilted.

Fresh rice noodles with beef

PREPARATION TIME: 10 MINUTES + 30 MINUTES MARINATING | TOTAL COOKING TIME: 15 MINUTES | SERVES 4–6

2 garlic cloves, crushed

2 teaspoons chopped fresh ginger

1 tablespoon oyster sauce

2 teaspoons soy sauce

500 g (1 lb 2 oz) beef, thinly sliced

oil, for cooking

1 kg (2 lb 4 oz) fresh rice noodle, sliced into 2 cm (¾ inch) strips

100 g (3½ oz/1 bunch) garlic chives, snipped into 2.5 cm (1 inch) lengths

2½ tablespoons oyster sauce, extra

3 teaspoons soy sauce, extra

1 teaspoon sugar

1 Combine the garlic, ginger, oyster and soy sauces, add the beef and toss to coat. Cover and refrigerate for 30 minutes.

2 Heat the wok until very hot, add 1 tablespoon of the oil and swirl it around to coat the side. Add half the beef and stir-fry for 5 minutes, or until cooked. Remove and repeat with the remaining beef. Add another tablespoon of oil, then add the noodles and stir-fry for 3–5 minutes, or until softened.

3 Add the garlic chives and stir-fry until just wilted. Stir in the extra oyster and soy sauces and sugar, return the beef to the wok and toss to heat through. Serve immediately.

Buy the fresh rice noodle as a block and cut it into thin strips.

Mix together the garlic, ginger, oyster and soy sauces to marinate the beef.

NUTRITION PER SERVE (6)

Protein 33 g; Fat 13 g; Carbohydrate 40 g; Dietary Fibre 1.5 g; Cholesterol 50 mg; 1295 kJ (310 Cal)

Thai braised beef with spinach and leeks

PREPARATION TIME: 10 MINUTES + 2 HOURS MARINATING | TOTAL COOKING TIME: 25 MINUTES | SERVES 4

400 g (14 oz) beef fillet
2 tablespoons light soy sauce
2 tablespoons fish sauce
oil, for cooking
4 coriander (cilantro) roots, finely chopped
1 very large handful coriander (cilantro) leaves
    and stems, chopped
2 teaspoons cracked black peppercorns
2 garlic cloves, crushed
1 tablespoon soft brown sugar
1 leek, sliced
20 English spinach leaves, stalks removed
3 tablespoons lime juice
shredded red capsicum (pepper), to garnish

1 Cut the beef into 2.5 cm (1 inch) thick pieces and place in a bowl. Place the sauces, 1 tablespoon of the oil, coriander, peppercorns, garlic and brown sugar in a blender and mix until smooth. Pour the marinade over the beef, cover and refrigerate for 2 hours.

2 Drain the beef, reserving the marinade. Heat the wok until very hot, add 1 tablespoon of the oil and swirl it around to coat the side. Stir-fry the beef in batches, browning well.

3 Return all the meat to the wok and add the reserved marinade and 125 ml (4 fl oz/ ½ cup) water. Reduce the heat and simmer for 8 minutes. Remove the meat and keep warm. Simmer the sauce for 10 minutes, then remove from the wok and set aside. Slice the beef into large bite-sized pieces.

4 Wipe out the wok and heat 1 tablespoon of the oil. Add the leek and stir-fry for 2 minutes. Add the spinach and cook for 30 seconds, or until wilted. Serve with the meat with the sauce poured over the top. Drizzle with lime juice and serve immediately with garnish.

NUTRITION PER SERVE
Protein 24 g; Fat 20 g; Carbohydrate 7 g; Dietary
Fibre 1.5 g; Cholesterol 67 mg; 1220 kJ (290 Cal)

Place the pieces of beef in a bowl and pour the marinade over the top.

Brown the beef in batches if necessary so that you don't overcrowd the wok.

Beef, vermicelli and Thai basil salad

PREPARATION TIME: 20 MINUTES | TOTAL COOKING TIME: 10–15 MINUTES | SERVES 4

125 g (4½ oz) dried rice vermicelli
600 g (1 lb 5 oz) rump steak
oil, for cooking
2–3 garlic cloves, thinly sliced
1 small red chilli, finely chopped
1 small red capsicum (pepper), thinly sliced
1 red onion, thinly sliced
2 very large handfuls coriander
    (cilantro) leaves
1 very large handful Thai basil leaves or
    green basil leaves

DRESSING
1–2 garlic cloves, crushed
1 red chilli, chopped
2 tablespoons soy sauce
2 tablespoons lime juice
1 tablespoon fish sauce
3 tablespoons grated palm sugar (jaggery)

1 Soak the noodles in hot water for 5 minutes, or until soft. Drain.

2 Combine the dressing ingredients, mix well and set aside.

3 Thinly slice the beef across the grain. Heat the wok until very hot, add 1 tablespoon of the oil and swirl it around to coat the side. Stir-fry the beef in 2–3 batches for 2 minutes, or until just brown, yet still pink in patches. (Ensure the wok is hot before each addition.) Remove all the beef and set aside.

4 Heat another tablespoon of the oil in the wok, then stir-fry the garlic, chilli, capsicum and onion for 2–3 minutes, or until soft but not browned.

5 Add the beef to the wok to just heat through quickly, then toss the vermicelli through the mixture. Pour on the dressing, and toss through the coriander and Thai basil leaves. Serve immediately.

NUTRITION PER SERVE
Protein 40 g; Fat 15 g; Carbohydrate 35 g; Dietary Fibre 2 g; Cholesterol 100 mg; 1795 kJ (425 Cal)

Using a large sharp knife, slice the rump steak thinly across the grain.

Stir-fry the beef in batches until it is just beginning to turn brown.

Add the beef and toss through the vermicelli until it is just heated through.

Asian peppered beef

PREPARATION TIME: 10 MINUTES + 2 HOURS MARINATING | TOTAL COOKING TIME: 12 MINUTES | SERVES 4

600 g (1 lb 5 oz) skirt steak, thinly sliced
2 garlic cloves, finely chopped
2 teaspoons finely chopped fresh ginger
2 onions, thinly sliced
2 tablespoons Chinese rice wine
1 teaspoon sesame oil
1 tablespoon soy sauce
1 tablespoon oyster sauce
2 teaspoons sugar
1 teaspoon sichuan peppercorns, crushed
1 tablespoon black peppercorns, crushed
2 spring onions (scallions), chopped into
    2.5 cm (1 inch) lengths, plus extra finely
    shredded spring onion, to garnish
oil, for cooking

1 Place the beef strips in a large bowl. Add the garlic, ginger, onion, rice wine, sesame oil, soy sauce, oyster sauce, sugar and peppercorns, and mix together well. Cover and marinate in the refrigerator for at least 2 hours.

2 Drain, discarding any excess liquid, and stir in the spring onion.

3 Heat the wok until very hot, add 1 tablespoon of the oil and swirl it around to coat the side. Add half the beef and stir-fry for 6 minutes, or until seared and cooked to your liking. Repeat with the rest of the beef. Serve immediately garnished with spring onion.

HINTS: *The wok needs to be searing hot for this recipe. The beef is easier to thinly slice if you put it in the freezer for half an hour beforehand.*

Crush the peppercorns in a mortar and pestle to release their flavour.

Chop the spring onions into short lengths for quick and even stir-frying.

NUTRITION PER SERVE
Protein 40 g; Fat 15 g; Carbohydrate 6 g; Dietary Fibre 1 g; Cholesterol 117 mg; 1400 kJ (335 Cal)

Thai red curry

PREPARATION TIME: 20 MINUTES | TOTAL COOKING TIME: 30–40 MINUTES | SERVES 4

oil, for cooking
2–6 teaspoons red curry paste, to taste
500 g (1 lb 2 oz) topside steak, thinly sliced
375 ml (13 fl oz/1½ cups) coconut milk
4 makrut (kaffir lime) leaves, roughly torn
100 g (3½ oz) pea eggplants or
     chopped eggplant
1½ tablespoons fish sauce
1½ tablespoons lime juice
2 teaspoons soft brown sugar
1 medium handful Thai basil or 1 very large
     handful coriander (cilantro) leaves

1   Heat the wok until very hot, add
1 tablespoon of the oil and swirl it around to
coat the side. Add the curry paste and stir for
1 minute over medium heat. Add the meat to the
wok in batches and stir-fry for 3 minutes, or until
brown. Remove all the meat from the wok and
set aside.

2   Add the coconut milk, makrut leaves and
250 ml (9 fl oz/1 cup) water to the wok, bring
to the boil and simmer for 12 minutes. Add the
eggplant and cook for 5–10 minutes, or until
tender. Return the beef to the wok and simmer
for 3 minutes.

3   Add the fish sauce, lime juice and brown
sugar to the wok. Add most of the basil or
coriander leaves, toss and serve immediately,
sprinkled with the remaining basil or
coriander leaves.

HINT: *The meat must be cooked for a short time
only so it remains tender.*

NOTE: *The makrut leaves are not meant to be
eaten as they are rather tough. However, no harm
will come to you if you do.*

Stir-fry the meat in batches for 3 minutes, or until
it is brown.

NUTRITION PER SERVE
Protein 7.5 g; Fat 13 g; Carbohydrate 3.5 g; Dietary
Fibre 1 g; Cholesterol 32 mg; 653 kJ (156 Cal)

Nasi goreng

PREPARATION TIME: 35 MINUTES | TOTAL COOKING TIME: 25–30 MINUTES | SERVES 4

2 eggs

oil, for cooking

3 garlic cloves, finely chopped

1 onion, finely chopped

2 red chillies, seeded and finely chopped

1 teaspoon dried shrimp paste

1 teaspoon coriander seeds

½ teaspoon sugar

200 g (7 oz) rump steak, thinly sliced

200 g (7 oz) peeled raw prawns (shrimp)

550 g (1 lb 4 oz/3 cups) cold cooked rice

2 teaspoons kecap manis (see NOTE, page 18)

1 tablespoon soy sauce

4 spring onions (scallions), finely chopped

lettuce and cucumber strips, to serve

3 tablespoons crisp-fried onions

1 Beat the eggs with a pinch of salt until foamy. Heat a frying pan and lightly brush with 1 tablespoon of the oil. Pour about one-quarter of the egg into the pan and cook for 1–2 minutes until the omelette sets. Flip and cook for 30 seconds. Remove from the pan and repeat with the remaining egg. When the omelettes are cold, gently roll up and shred finely.

2 Process the garlic, onion, chilli, shrimp paste, coriander and sugar in a food processor, or pound using a mortar and pestle, until a paste forms.

3 Heat a wok over high heat, add 1 tablespoon of the oil and fry the paste for 1 minute, or until fragrant. Add the steak and prawns and stir-fry until they change colour. Add 2 tablespoons of the oil and the rice. Stir-fry, breaking up any lumps, until the rice is heated through. Add the kecap manis, soy sauce and spring onion and stir-fry for another minute. Serve immediately, on a bed of lettuce and cucumber, garnished with the omelette strips and crisp-fried onions.

NUTRITION PER SERVE
Protein 20 g; Fat 23 g; Carbohydrate 44 g; Dietary Fibre 3.5 g; Cholesterol 125 mg; 1942 kJ (465 Cal)

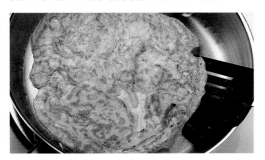
Cook the omelette for 1–2 minutes, or until it has set. Then turn it over and cook the other side.

Process the garlic, onion, chilli, shrimp paste, coriander and sugar into a paste.

Quickly stir-fry the beef and prawns until they change colour.

Thai green curry

PREPARATION TIME: 20 MINUTES | TOTAL COOKING TIME: 30–35 MINUTES | SERVES 4

oil, for cooking
1 large onion, chopped
1–2 tablespoons green curry paste, to taste
500 g (1 lb 2 oz) round or blade steak, thickly
    sliced
185 ml (6 fl oz/¾ cup) coconut milk
6 makrut (kaffir lime) leaves (see NOTE,
    page 33)
90 g (3¼ oz) pea eggplants
2 tablespoons fish sauce
1 teaspoon soft brown sugar
2 teaspoons finely grated lime zest
1 very large handful coriander (cilantro) leaves
1 large handful basil leaves

1 Heat the wok until very hot, add
1 tablespoon of the oil and swirl it around to
coat the side. Add the onion and curry paste
and stir over medium heat for 2 minutes, or
until fragrant.

2 Add the beef in two batches and stir-fry until
brown. Return all the meat to the wok. Add the
coconut milk, makrut leaves and 3 tablespoons
water. Bring to the boil, reduce the heat and
simmer for 10 minutes. Add the eggplants and
cook for 10 minutes, or until tender.

3 Add the fish sauce, brown sugar and lime
zest and toss together well. Stir in the coriander
and basil leaves just before serving.

Stir the curry paste and onion over medium heat for 2 minutes, or until fragrant.

After cooking the beef for 10 minutes, add the pea eggplants to the wok.

NUTRITION PER SERVE
Protein 28 g; Fat 12 g; Carbohydrate 5 g; Dietary
Fibre 1.5 g; Cholesterol 66 mg; 1010 kJ (240 Cal)

Beef with bok choy

PREPARATION TIME: 20 MINUTES | TOTAL COOKING TIME: 10 MINUTES | SERVES 4

1 bunch bok choy (pak choy)
(see VARIATION)
oil, for cooking
2 garlic cloves, crushed
250 g (9 oz) rump steak, thinly sliced
2 tablespoons soy sauce
1 tablespoon sweet sherry
2 tablespoons chopped basil
2 teaspoons sesame oil

1 Wash the bok choy and drain. Cut the leaves into wide strips and the stems into thin strips. Heat the wok until very hot, add 1 tablespoon of the oil and swirl to coat the side. Add the garlic and stir-fry for 30 seconds.

2 Add another tablespoon of the oil to the wok and add the meat in batches. Stir-fry for 3 minutes over high heat, until the meat has browned but not cooked through. Remove from the wok.

3 Add the bok choy to the wok and stir-fry for 30 seconds, or until just wilted. Return the meat and add the soy sauce and sherry. Stir-fry for 2–3 minutes, or until the meat is tender.

4 Add the basil and sesame oil and toss well. Serve immediately.

VARIATION: *The Asian vegetable choy sum has a similar flavour to bok choy and could also be used for this recipe. It has a longer leaf and shorter stem. Baby bok choy could also be used for this recipe.*

NUTRITION PER SERVE
Protein 60 g; Fat 40 g; Carbohydrate 0.5 g; Dietary Fibre 1 g; Cholesterol 42 mg; 790 kJ (190 Cal)

Cut the leaves of bok choy into wide strips and cut the stalks into thin strips.

Stir-fry the bok choy briefly until the leaves have just begun to wilt.

Beef with leeks and snow peas

PREPARATION TIME: 25 MINUTES | TOTAL COOKING TIME: 15 MINUTES | SERVES 4

oil, for cooking

375 g (13 oz) rump steak, very thinly sliced

2–3 garlic cloves, finely chopped

1 lemongrass stem, white part only,
   finely chopped

1 leek, white part only, thinly sliced

2 celery stalks, thickly sliced

8 spring onions (scallions), diagonally sliced

150 g (5½ oz) snow peas (mangetouts),
   halved

100 g (3½ oz) oyster mushrooms, halved

2 tablespoons kecap manis (see NOTE,
   page 18)

2 tablespoons sweet chilli sauce

2 tablespoons lime or lemon juice

3 makrut (kaffir lime) leaves, shredded
   (see HINT)

1 tablespoon fish sauce, or to taste

NUTRITION PER SERVE
Protein 25 g; Fat 13 g; Carbohydrate 8.5 g; Dietary
Fibre 5 g; Cholesterol 65 mg; 1065 kJ (255 Cal)

1 Heat the wok until very hot, add 1 tablespoon of the oil and swirl it around to coat the side. Stir-fry the beef strips, garlic and lemongrass in two or three batches over high heat for 2–3 minutes, or until the beef is browned. Remove all the beef mixture from the wok.

2 Reheat the wok, add 1 tablespoon of the oil and stir-fry the leek, celery and spring onion for 2 minutes. Add the snow peas and oyster mushrooms, and stir-fry for 1–2 minutes, or until tender. Remove the vegetables from the wok and set aside.

3 Add the combined kecap manis, chilli sauce and lime or lemon juice to the wok, and bring to the boil. Return all the beef and vegetables to the wok and stir-fry for 1–2 minutes, or until the beef has just heated through and everything is well coated with the sauce. Toss the shredded makrut leaves through the mixture and sprinkle with the fish sauce, to taste. Serve at once.

HINT: *If makrut leaves are not available, sprinkle the stir-fry with 3 tablespoons chopped fresh basil leaves just before serving. (If you chop and add them earlier, they tend to turn black.)*

Finely chop the white part of the lemongrass stem, discarding the green part.

Stir-fry the beef, garlic and lemongrass until the beef browns.

Pork

Sweet and sour pork

PREPARATION TIME: 25 MINUTES + 30 MINUTES MARINATING | TOTAL COOKING TIME: 20 MINUTES | SERVES 4

500 g (1 lb 2 oz) pork fillet, thickly sliced

2 tablespoons cornflour (cornstarch)

1 tablespoon sweet sherry

1 tablespoon soy sauce

1 tablespoon sugar

oil, for cooking

1 large onion, thinly sliced

2 small carrots, thinly sliced

1 small Lebanese (short) cucumber, seeded
and chopped

5 spring onions (scallions), cut into
short lengths

440 g (15½ oz) can pineapple pieces in
natural juice, drained, 4 tablespoons
juice reserved

60 ml (2 fl oz/¼ cup) white vinegar

NUTRITION PER SERVE
Protein 25 g; Fat 12 g; Carbohydrate 25 g; Dietary
Fibre 4 g; Cholesterol 50 mg; 1325 kJ (315 Cal)

1   Place the pork in a shallow glass or ceramic bowl. Combine the cornflour with the sherry, soy sauce and half the sugar and pour into the bowl. Cover and refrigerate for 30 minutes.

2   Drain the pork, reserving the marinade. Heat the wok until very hot, add 2 tablespoons of the oil and swirl to coat the side. Stir-fry half the pork over high heat for 4–5 minutes, or until the pork is golden brown and just cooked. Remove from the wok, add more oil if necessary and repeat with the remaining pork. Remove all the pork from the wok.

3   Reheat the wok, add 1 tablespoon of the oil and stir-fry the onion over high heat for 3–4 minutes, or until slightly softened. Add the carrot, and cook for 3–4 minutes, or until tender. Stir in the reserved marinade, cucumber, spring onion, pineapple, vinegar, ½ teaspoon salt, remaining sugar and the reserved pineapple juice.

4   Bring to the boil and simmer for 2–3 minutes, or until the sauce has thickened slightly. Return the pork to the wok and toss until the pork is heated through. Serve immediately.

Peel the carrots, if necessary, and cut them into thin diagonal slices.

Halve the cucumber lengthways and scoop out the seeds with a teaspoon.

Stir-fry the pork until it is golden brown and just cooked through.

Pork with pumpkin and cashew nuts

PREPARATION TIME: 20 MINUTES | TOTAL COOKING TIME: 20 MINUTES | SERVES 4

2–3 tablespoons oil

90 g (3¼ oz/½ cup) cashew nuts

750 g (1 lb 10 oz) pork neck, thinly sliced

500 g (1 lb 2 oz) pumpkin (winter squash), cubed

1 tablespoon grated fresh ginger

80 ml (2½ fl oz/⅓ cup) chicken stock

60 ml (2 fl oz/¼ cup) dry sherry

1½ tablespoons soy sauce

½ teaspoon cornflour (cornstarch)

500 g (1 lb 2 oz/1 bunch) baby bok choy (pak choy), chopped

1–2 tablespoons coriander (cilantro) leaves

1 Heat a wok until very hot, add 1 tablespoon of the oil and swirl to coat the side of the wok. Stir-fry the cashews for 1–2 minutes, or until browned. Drain on paper towels.

2 Reheat the wok, add a little extra oil and swirl to coat. Stir-fry the pork in batches for 5 minutes, or until lightly browned. Remove from the wok. Add 1 tablespoon oil to the wok and stir-fry the pumpkin and ginger for 3 minutes, or until lightly browned. Add the stock, sherry and soy sauce, and cook for 3 minutes, or until the pumpkin is tender.

3 Blend the cornflour with 1 teaspoon water until smooth, add to the wok and stir until the mixture boils and thickens. Return the pork and cashews to the wok and add the bok choy and coriander. Stir until the bok choy has just wilted. Serve immediately.

Stir-fry the cashew nuts for 1–2 minutes, or until they are just browned.

Reheat the wok and brown the pork in batches so that it fries rather than stews.

NUTRITION PER SERVE
Protein 46 g; Fat 28 g; Carbohydrate 15 g; Dietary Fibre 8 g; Cholesterol 75 mg; 2112 kJ (505 Cal)

Chinese pork with broccoli

PREPARATION TIME: 10 MINUTES | TOTAL COOKING TIME: 10 MINUTES | SERVES 4

1.6 kg (3 lb 8 oz) Chinese broccoli, cut into
    short lengths
1 tablespoon peanut oil
2.5 cm (1 inch) piece fresh ginger, peeled and
    cut into matchsticks
2 garlic cloves, crushed
500 g (1 lb 2 oz) Chinese barbecued pork,
    thinly sliced
60 ml (2 fl oz/¼ cup) chicken or
    vegetable stock
60 ml (2 fl oz/¼ cup) oyster sauce
1 tablespoon kecap manis (see NOTE,
    page 18)

1 Place the broccoli in a steamer over a wok of simmering water and cook for 5 minutes, or until just tender but still crisp.

2 Drain the wok, dry thoroughly and heat until very hot. Add the peanut oil and swirl to coat. Add the ginger and garlic and stir-fry for 30 seconds, or until fragrant. Add the broccoli and pork and toss to coat.

3 Mix together the stock, oyster sauce and kecap manis and add to the wok. Toss thoroughly until heated through and then serve immediately.

NUTRITION PER SERVE
Protein 30 g; Fat 7 g; Carbohydrate 4.5 g; Dietary
Fibre 2 g; Cholesterol 60 mg; 886 kJ (212 Cal)

Peel the piece of fresh ginger and then cut it into thin matchsticks.

Put the broccoli in a steamer over a wok of simmering water and cook until tender.

Stir-fry the ginger and garlic, then add the broccoli and pork to the wok.

Sichuan pork with capsicum

PREPARATION TIME: 30 MINUTES | TOTAL COOKING TIME: 10 MINUTES | SERVES 4–6

1½ tablespoons cornflour (cornstarch)

1 tablespoon sichuan peppercorns, ground

2 egg whites, beaten

500 g (1 lb 2 oz) pork fillet, thinly sliced

2 tablespoons peanut oil, plus
      1 teaspoon, extra

1 red capsicum (pepper), thinly sliced

2 spring onions (scallions), sliced into
      short lengths, plus extra finely shredded
      spring onion, to garnish

2 teaspoons chilli oil

4 star anise

2 garlic cloves, crushed

2 teaspoons finely chopped fresh ginger

2 tablespoons oyster sauce

2 tablespoons Chinese rice wine

2 tablespoons soy sauce

½ teaspoon sesame oil

2 teaspoons sugar

1   Place the cornflour, peppercorns, egg whites and ½ teaspoon salt in a bowl. Mix well, then add the pork and toss to coat.

2   Heat a wok until very hot, add 1 teaspoon peanut oil and swirl to coat the side of the wok. Add the capsicum and spring onion and stir-fry for 1 minute. Remove from the wok.

3   Add 1 tablespoon peanut oil to the wok and swirl to coat the side of the wok. Add half the pork and stir-fry for 2 minutes, or until sealed. Remove. Repeat with the remaining oil and pork.

4   Add the chilli oil to the wok and swirl to coat. Add the star anise and stir-fry for 30 seconds, then add the garlic and ginger and stir-fry for another few seconds.

5   Combine the oyster sauce, rice wine, soy sauce, sesame oil and sugar, add to the wok and cook for 30 seconds. Return the pork to the wok and stir-fry for 1 minute, then stir in the vegetables and serve, topped with finely shredded spring onion.

NUTRITION PER SERVE (6)
Protein 20 g; Fat 11 g; Carbohydrate 4 g; Dietary Fibre 0.5 g; Cholesterol 40 mg; 865 kJ (207 Cal)

Mix together the cornflour, peppercorns, egg whites and salt, then add the pork.

Stir-fry the capsicum and spring onion in the peanut oil for 1 minute.

Add half of the pork to the wok so that the pork doesn't overcrowd and stew in its juices.

Sesame pork

PREPARATION TIME: 10 MINUTES | TOTAL COOKING TIME: 20 MINUTES | SERVES 4

2 tablespoons sesame seeds
3 tablespoons peanut oil
600 g (1 lb 5 oz) pork fillet, thinly sliced
2 tablespoons hoisin sauce
2 tablespoons teriyaki sauce
2 teaspoons cornflour (cornstarch)
2 teaspoons sesame oil
8 spring onions (scallions), sliced on
    the diagonal, plus extra finely shredded
    spring onion, to garnish
2 garlic cloves, crushed
2 teaspoons finely grated fresh ginger
2 carrots, cut into matchsticks
200 g (7 oz) snake beans, cut into short lengths

1   Preheat the oven to moderate 180°C (350°F/ Gas 4). Place the sesame seeds on an oven tray and bake for 5 minutes, or until browned.

2   Heat a wok until very hot, add 1 tablespoon peanut oil and swirl to coat. Add half the pork and stir-fry for 3 minutes, or until browned. Remove. Repeat with the remaining pork. Remove.

3   Combine the hoisin and teriyaki sauces, cornflour and 1 tablespoon water and mix until smooth.

4   Reheat the wok until very hot, add the remaining peanut oil and the sesame oil and swirl to coat the side. Add the spring onion, garlic and ginger, and stir-fry for 1 minute, or until fragrant.

5   Add the carrot and beans, and stir-fry for 3 minutes, or until almost cooked but still crunchy. Return the pork to the wok, add the cornflour mixture and stir until the sauce boils and thickens. Simmer for 2 minutes, or until the meat is tender and the vegetables are just cooked. Toss through the sesame seeds and serve immediately garnished with spring onion.

NUTRITION PER SERVE
Protein 38 g; Fat 27 g; Carbohydrate 7.5 g; Dietary Fibre 4.5 g; Cholesterol 75 mg; 1766 kJ (420 Cal)

Cut the snake beans into shorter lengths for easy stir-frying.

Cook the pork in two batches, so that it fries rather than stews.

Pork and green beans with ginger sauce

PREPARATION TIME: 15 MINUTES | TOTAL COOKING TIME: 10 MINUTES | SERVES 4

185 ml (6 fl oz/¾ cup) soy sauce
4 tablespoons white or rice wine vinegar
1 teaspoon sugar
pinch of dried chilli flakes
3 teaspoons cornflour (cornstarch)
600 g (1 lb 5 oz) pork fillet, trimmed and
    thinly sliced
2 tablespoons peanut oil
350 g (12 oz) green beans, cut into
    short lengths
2 garlic cloves, chopped
2 tablespoons grated fresh ginger

1   Place the soy sauce, vinegar, sugar, chilli flakes, cornflour and 80 ml (2½ fl oz/⅓ cup) water in a bowl and mix well. Add the pork and toss to coat well.

2   Heat a wok over high heat, add half the peanut oil and swirl to coat the side. Drain the pork, reserving the liquid, and add to the wok. Stir-fry over high heat for 1–2 minutes, or until brown. Remove the pork from the wok.

3   Heat the remaining oil, add the beans and stir-fry for 3–4 minutes. Add the garlic and ginger and stir-fry for 1 minute, or until fragrant. Return the pork and any juices to the pan and add the reserved marinade. Bring to the boil and cook, stirring, for 1–2 minutes, or until slightly thickened. Serve with steamed rice.

NOTE: *Rice wine vinegar is made by oxidising beer or wine made from fermented rice starch.*

Add the pork to the wok and stir-fry until the meat is browned.

Heat the remaining oil in the wok and stir-fry the green beans.

NUTRITION PER SERVE
Protein 51 g; Fat 23 g; Carbohydrate 11 g; Dietary
Fibre 3.5 g; Cholesterol 100 mg; 1917 kJ (458 Cal)

Udon noodles with ginger pork and pickles

PREPARATION TIME: 30 MINUTES + 20 MINUTES MARINATING | TOTAL COOKING TIME: 25 MINUTES | SERVES 4

10 cm (4 inch) piece fresh ginger, peeled
pinch of sugar
200 g (7 oz) pork loin
500 g (1 lb 2 oz) dried udon noodles
2 tablespoons cornflour (cornstarch)
2 tablespoons oil
150 g (5½ oz) broccoli, cut into long thin
    florets
100 g (3½ oz) Chinese pickled vegetables,
    thinly sliced
4 spring onions (scallions), sliced
3 tablespoons soy sauce
3 tablespoons mirin
1 Lebanese (short) cucumber, halved and
    thinly sliced
2 tablespoons toasted sesame seeds

NUTRITION PER SERVE
Protein 30 g; Fat 15 g; Carbohydrate 105 g; Dietary
Fibre 4 g; Cholesterol 25 mg; 2880 kJ (685 Cal)

1 Slice one-third of the ginger paper-thin and place in a bowl, then finely grate the rest. Squeeze the grated ginger over the ginger slices and discard the dry pulp. Season well with salt, pepper and the sugar.

2 Cut the pork into 5 cm (2 inch) strips. Add to the ginger. Mix well and leave to marinate for 20 minutes.

3 Cook the noodles in plenty of salted boiling water for 12 minutes, or until tender. Drain, rinse and set aside.

4 Remove the ginger slices from the pork. Scatter the cornflour over the pork and mix well. Heat half the oil in a wok over medium–high heat. Quickly stir-fry the pork until golden, adding the ginger at the end. Remove and set aside.

5 Heat the remaining oil and stir-fry the broccoli, pickles and spring onion for 30 seconds. Add 1 tablespoon of water, then cover and steam for 30 seconds.

6 Add the noodles, soy sauce and mirin to the wok and toss well until heated through. Add the pork and ginger and toss well. Divide among bowls, garnish with cucumber and sesame seeds and serve at once.

Buy the Chinese pickled vegetables from Asian food stores and slice them thinly.

Slice a third of the ginger as thinly as you can, then grate the rest.

Add the noodles, soy sauce and mirin to the wok and toss well.

Black bean pork with bok choy

PREPARATION TIME: 20 MINUTES | TOTAL COOKING TIME: 10 MINUTES | SERVES 4

400 g (14 oz) lean pork leg steak
1 tablespoon canned salted black beans, rinsed
500 g (1 lb 2 oz/1 bunch) baby bok choy
   (pak choy)
2 teaspoons sesame oil
2 onions, thinly sliced
2 garlic cloves, thinly chopped
2–3 teaspoons chopped fresh ginger
1 red capsicum (pepper), thinly sliced
90 g (3¼ oz/½ cup) water chestnuts,
   thinly sliced
2 tablespoons oyster sauce
1 tablespoon soy sauce
2 teaspoons fish sauce

1 Slice the pork steak into strips, cutting across the grain. Roughly chop the beans. Separate the leaves of the bok choy, trim away the tough ends and shred the leaves.

2 Heat half the sesame oil in a large wok. Cook the onion, garlic and ginger over high heat for 3–4 minutes. Add the capsicum and cook for 2–3 minutes. Remove from the wok. Heat the remaining sesame oil and stir-fry the pork in batches over high heat.

3 Return all the pork to the wok along with the onion mixture, black beans, shredded bok choy, water chestnuts and oyster, soy and fish sauces. Toss quickly to combine the ingredients, lower the heat, cover and steam for 3–4 minutes, or until the bok choy has just wilted. Serve immediately.

Separate the leaves of the bok choy and then trim the tough ends.

Stir-fry the pork strips in batches over high heat until brown.

NUTRITION PER SERVE
Protein 30 g; Fat 3 g; Carbohydrate 20 g; Dietary Fibre 3.5 g; Cholesterol 55 mg; 910 kJ (215 Cal)

Thai red pork and pumpkin curry

PREPARATION TIME: 20 MINUTES | TOTAL COOKING TIME: 25 MINUTES | SERVES 4

1 tablespoon oil
1–2 tablespoons red curry paste, to taste
500 g (1 lb 2 oz) lean pork, cubed
250 ml (9 fl oz/1 cup) coconut milk
350 g (12 oz) pumpkin (winter squash), peeled
   and cubed
6 makrut (kaffir lime) leaves (see NOTE,
   page 33)
60 ml (2 fl oz/¼ cup) coconut cream
1 tablespoon fish sauce
1 teaspoon soft brown sugar
2 red chillies, thinly sliced

1 Heat the oil in a wok, add the curry paste and stir for 1 minute.

2 Add the pork to the wok and stir-fry over medium-high heat until golden brown. Add the coconut milk, pumpkin, makrut leaves and 125 ml (4 fl oz/½ cup) water, reduce the heat and simmer for 15 minutes, or until the pork and pumpkin are tender.

3 Add the coconut cream, fish sauce and brown sugar and stir to combine. Scatter the chilli over the top to serve.

NUTRITION PER SERVE
Protein 30 g; Fat 11 g; Carbohydrate 9 g; Dietary
Fibre 1.5 g; Cholesterol 62 mg; 1085 kJ (260 Cal)

Add the curry paste to the hot oil and stir with a wooden spoon for 1 minute.

Add the pork pieces to the wok and stir-fry over medium–high heat until golden brown.

Add the coconut cream, fish sauce and brown sugar to the wok and stir well.

Thai crispy fried noodles

PREPARATION TIME: 30 MINUTES | TOTAL COOKING TIME: 20 MINUTES | SERVES 4

500 ml (17 fl oz/2 cups) oil, for frying
100 g (3½ oz) deep-fried tofu puffs, cut
    into strips
100 g (3½ oz) rice vermicelli
2 garlic cloves, finely chopped
5 cm (2 inch) piece fresh ginger, grated
150 g (5½ oz) minced (ground) pork
100 g (3½ oz) raw prawn (shrimp) meat,
    finely chopped
1 tablespoon white vinegar
2 tablespoons fish sauce
2 tablespoons soft brown sugar
2 tablespoons chilli sauce
1 teaspoon chopped red chillies
2 small knobs pickled garlic, chopped
¼ bunch fresh garlic chives, snipped
2 very large handfuls coriander
    (cilantro) leaves

1 Heat the oil in a wok, add the tofu in two batches and cook for 1 minute, or until golden and crisp. Remove from the wok and leave to drain.

2 Add the vermicelli to the oil in several batches, cooking for 10 seconds, or until puffed and crisp. Remove immediately to prevent the vermicelli absorbing too much oil. Drain on paper towels and cool.

3 Drain all but 1 tablespoon of the oil from the wok. Reheat the wok over high heat and add the garlic, ginger, minced pork and prawn meat. Stir-fry for 2 minutes, or until golden brown. Add the vinegar, fish sauce, brown sugar, chilli sauce and chillies and stir until the mixture comes to the boil.

4 Just before serving, add the noodles and tofu to the wok and toss thoroughly. Quickly toss through the pickled garlic, chives and coriander and serve immediately.

NUTRITION PER SERVE
Protein 8.5 g; Fat 13 g; Carbohydrate 17 g; Dietary
Fibre 2.5 g; Cholesterol 37 mg; 900 kJ (230 Cal)

Cook the tofu for 2 minutes, until golden brown. Remove with a wire mesh strainer.

Add the vermicelli to the wok in batches and cook until puffed and crisp.

Add the chopped garlic, grated ginger, minced pork and prawn meat to the wok.

Spicy sausage stir-fry

PREPARATION TIME: 40 MINUTES | TOTAL COOKING TIME: 15 MINUTES | SERVES 4

2 tablespoons oil
500 g (1 lb 2 oz) potato, cubed
500 g (1 lb 2 oz) orange sweet potato, cubed
6 chorizo sausages, diagonally sliced
2 garlic cloves, thinly sliced
1 red onion, cut into wedges
200 g (7 oz) broccoli, chopped
1 red capsicum (pepper), cut into short
    thick strips
125 ml (4 fl oz/½ cup) tomato passata
    (puréed tomatoes)
2 tablespoons chopped fresh flat-leaf (Italian)
    parsley, and leaves, to garnish

1   Heat the wok until very hot, add the oil
and swirl it around to coat the side. Stir-fry the
potato and sweet potato over medium heat until
tender and golden. Remove and drain on paper
towels, then place on a serving plate and cover to
keep warm.

2   Add the sausage to the wok and stir-fry in
batches over high heat for 3–4 minutes, or until
crisp. Remove and drain on paper towels.

3   Add the garlic and onion to the wok and
stir-fry for 2 minutes, or until the onion softens.
Add the broccoli and capsicum and stir-fry for
1 minute. Return the sausage to the wok, add the
passata and toss to combine. Add the parsley and
season with salt and black pepper. Toss well and
serve on top of the stir-fried potato, garnished
with parsley.

Peel the skin from the sweet potato and cut the
flesh into cubes.

Chorizo is a spicy Spanish sausage. Cut the chorizo
into thick diagonal slices.

NUTRITION PER SERVE
Protein 20 g; Fat 30 g; Carbohydrate 40 g; Dietary
Fibre 8 g; Cholesterol 55 mg; 2390 kJ (570 Cal)

Larb (spicy Thai pork salad)

PREPARATION TIME: 20 MINUTES | TOTAL COOKING TIME: 8 MINUTES | SERVES 4–6

1 tablespoon oil
2 lemongrass stems, white part only,
    thinly sliced
2 fresh green chillies, finely chopped
500 g (1 lb 2 oz) lean minced (ground) pork
60 ml (2 fl oz/¼ cup) lime juice
2 teaspoons finely grated lime zest
2–6 teaspoons chilli sauce, to taste
lettuce leaves, for serving
1 large handful coriander (cilantro) leaves
1 medium handful small mint leaves
1 small onion, very thinly sliced
50 g (1¾ oz/⅓ cup) roasted unsalted
    peanuts, chopped
3 tablespoons crisp-fried garlic

1   Heat the oil in a wok. Add the lemongrass, chilli and pork. Stir-fry, breaking up any lumps with a fork or wooden spoon, over high heat for 6 minutes, or until cooked through. Transfer to a bowl and allow to cool.

2   Add the lime juice and zest and the chilli sauce to the cooled pork mixture. Arrange the lettuce leaves on a serving plate. Stir most of the coriander and mint leaves, onion, peanuts and fried garlic through the pork mixture. Spoon over the lettuce and sprinkle the rest of the leaves, onion, peanuts and garlic over the top to serve.

NUTRITION PER SERVE (6)
Protein 22 g; Fat 8.5 g; Carbohydrate 3.5 g; Dietary Fibre 2 g; Cholesterol 40 mg; 760 kJ (180 Cal)

Finely slice the white part of the lemongrass with a sharp knife.

Stir-fry the lemongrass, chilli and pork, breaking up the meat as it cooks.

Peppered coconut pork fillet

PREPARATION TIME: 40 MINUTES | TOTAL COOKING TIME: 20 MINUTES | SERVES 4

1 tablespoon cumin seeds

1 tablespoon coriander seeds

1 teaspoon black peppercorns

100 g (3½ oz/1⅔ cups) shredded coconut

2 tablespoons cornflour (cornstarch)

600 g (1 lb 5 oz) pork fillet

oil, for cooking

125 ml (4 fl oz/½ cup) thick coconut cream

60 ml (2 fl oz/¼ cup) lime juice

2 tablespoons chopped coriander (cilantro) and leaves, to garnish

NUTRITION PER SERVE
Protein 35 g; Fat 35 g; Carbohydrate 8 g; Dietary Fibre 4 g; Cholesterol 75 mg; 2030 kJ (485 Cal)

1   Heat the wok, add the cumin and coriander seeds and dry-fry over low heat, shaking the wok regularly, for 3 minutes, or until the seeds are fragrant. Place in a mortar and pestle with the peppercorns, and pound until finely ground. Alternatively, process in a spice mill or small food processor. Combine with the coconut and cornflour, mixing well.

2   Trim the pork of any fat and cut into slices about 1 cm (½ inch) thick, then cut across in half. Coat each slice in the spice mixture, using your fingertips to press the mixture on.

3   Reheat the wok until very hot, add 1 tablespoon of the oil and swirl it around to coat the side. Stir-fry the pork in three or four batches for about 2 minutes, or until it is golden brown and just cooked. Reheat the wok in between batches, adding more oil when necessary. Remove all the pork from the wok and keep warm.

4   Drain any oil from the wok and pour in the coconut cream and lime juice. Add the coriander and ¼ teaspoon salt, to taste. Bring to a vigorous boil, stirring for 1 minute. Add the pork and toss to heat through and combine with the sauce. Serve immediately, sprinkled with coriander leaves.

Dry-fry the cumin and coriander seeds in the wok until they are fragrant.

Grind the seeds with the peppercorns in a mortar and pestle.

Press the spice mixture onto the pork slices to coat them.

Citrus chilli pork with cashew nuts

PREPARATION TIME: 20 MINUTES | TOTAL COOKING TIME: 12 MINUTES | SERVES 4

2 tablespoons oil
375 g (13 oz) pork fillet, thinly sliced
2 small red chillies, seeded and finely chopped
6 spring onions (scallions), chopped
1 tablespoon mild curry paste
2 tablespoons fish sauce
1–2 tablespoons lime juice
2 teaspoons crushed palm sugar (jaggery)
2 teaspoons cornflour (cornstarch)
½–1 teaspoon soy sauce
50 g (1¾ oz/⅓ cup) roasted unsalted cashews
shredded lime zest, to garnish

1 Heat the wok until very hot, add the oil and swirl it around to coat the side. Stir-fry the pork slices, chilli and spring onion in batches over high heat for 2 minutes, or until the pork just changes colour. Stir in the curry paste and stir-fry for 1 minute. Remove from the wok and set aside.

2 Combine the fish sauce, lime juice, sugar and cornflour with 125 ml (4 fl oz/½ cup) water. Pour into the wok and stir for 1 minute, or until heated through and slightly thickened. Return the meat to the wok and toss vigorously until heated through.

3 Stir in the soy sauce, to taste, and cashews. Top with the lime zest.

NUTRITION PER SERVE
Protein 25 g; Fat 20 g; Carbohydrate 9 g; Dietary Fibre 1 g; Cholesterol 45 mg; 1215 kJ (290 Cal)

Fried noodles with mushrooms and barbecued pork

PREPARATION TIME: 30 MINUTES | TOTAL COOKING TIME: 6 MINUTES | SERVES 4

8 dried Chinese mushrooms
2 tablespoons oil
4 garlic cloves, chopped
5 cm (2 inch) piece fresh ginger, grated
1–2 teaspoons chopped red chillies, to taste
100 g (3½ oz) Chinese barbecued pork, cut
    into small pieces
200 g (7 oz) fresh egg noodles
2 teaspoons fish sauce
2 tablespoons lime juice
2 teaspoons soft brown sugar
2 tablespoons crisp-fried garlic
2 tablespoons crisp-fried onion
chilli flakes
shredded spring onion (scallion), to garnish

1   Soak the mushrooms in hot water for
20 minutes. Drain and cut them into quarters.

2   Heat the oil in a large wok. Add the garlic,
ginger and chilli and stir-fry for 1 minute over
high heat. Add the pork and stir for 1 minute.

3   Add the egg noodles and mushrooms and
toss well. Sprinkle the fish sauce, lime juice and
soft brown sugar over the pork and then toss
quickly, cover and steam for 30 seconds. Sprinkle
the fried garlic and onion, chilli flakes and spring
onion over the top before serving.

NUTRITION PER SERVE
Protein 16 g; Fat 12 g; Carbohydrate 40 g; Dietary
Fibre 3 g; Cholesterol 32 mg; 1375 kJ (328 Cal)

Add the pork pieces to the wok and stir with a
wooden spoon for 1 minute.

Cover the wok and allow the noodles to steam for
30 seconds.

San choy bau

PREPARATION TIME: 20 MINUTES + 30 MINUTES FOR LETTUCE CRISPING | TOTAL COOKING TIME: 10 MINUTES | SERVES 4–6

1–2 large lettuces
1 tablespoon oil
3 spring onions (scallions), chopped
2 teaspoons red curry paste
100 g (3½ oz) minced (ground) pork
100 g (3½ oz) small raw prawns (shrimp),
    peeled and deveined
3 tablespoons coconut milk
1–2 teaspoons chopped red chillies
2 teaspoons fish sauce
1 teaspoon soft brown sugar
2 teaspoons grated lime zest
3 tablespoons finely chopped roasted
    unsalted peanuts

1 Separate the lettuce leaves, wash them and pat dry, then wrap in a dry tea towel (dish towel) and refrigerate for about 30 minutes to crisp up.

2 Heat the oil in a wok and swirl to coat the side. Add the spring onion and curry paste and stir-fry for 2 minutes over medium heat.

3 Add the minced pork and stir-fry until browned. Add the prawns, coconut milk and chillies and stir-fry for 3 minutes.

4 Add the fish sauce, brown sugar and lime zest and stir well. Stir in the peanuts, then leave to cool for 15 minutes. Place a spoonful of spicy pork on each lettuce leaf—the parcels can be rolled for easy eating.

HINT: *The filling must be cooled so that all liquid will be absorbed, making it moist and succulent.*

NUTRITION PER SERVE (6)
Protein 10 g; Fat 8.5 g; Carbohydrate 3 g; Dietary Fibre 2 g; Cholesterol 33 mg; 535 kJ (128 Cal)

Separate the lettuce leaves, wash and pat dry, then wrap in a tea towel and refrigerate.

Use a wooden spoon to stir the spring onions and curry paste in the wok.

Add the prawns, coconut milk and chillies to the wok and stir-fry for 3 minutes.

Pork ball curry with egg noodles

PREPARATION TIME: 15 MINUTES | TOTAL COOKING TIME: 20 MINUTES | SERVES 4

200 g (7 oz) minced (ground) pork
3 garlic cloves, chopped
2 lemongrass stems, white part only,
    finely chopped
2.5 cm (1 inch) piece ginger, grated
1 tablespoon oil
1–2 tablespoons green curry paste, to taste
375 ml (13 fl oz/1½ cups) coconut milk
2 tablespoons fish sauce
2 teaspoons soft brown sugar
1 medium handful chopped Thai basil leaves
200 g (7 oz) fresh egg noodles
sliced spring onions (scallions), coriander
    (cilantro) leaves and sliced chillies, to serve

1   Finely chop the minced pork with a cleaver
or large knife. Combine the pork, garlic,
lemongrass and ginger in a bowl and mix
thoroughly. Form teaspoonfuls into small balls.

2   Heat the oil in a wok, add the curry paste and
cook over low heat, stirring constantly, for
1 minute, or until fragrant. Add the coconut milk
and 250 ml (9 fl oz/1 cup) water to the wok. Stir
until boiling, then reduce the heat and simmer
for 5 minutes. Add the pork balls and simmer for
5 minutes, or until cooked. Add the fish sauce,
brown sugar and Thai basil.

3   Cook the noodles in boiling water for
4 minutes, or until tender, then drain. Toss
with the pork balls and curry sauce and then
serve immediately, as the noodles will soak up
the sauce. Scatter spring onions, coriander and
chillies over the top.

Mix together the minced pork, garlic, lemongrass and ginger and form into meatballs.

Add the coconut milk and water to the wok and stir until boiling.

NUTRITION PER SERVE
Protein 20 g; Fat 25 g; Carbohydrate 42 g; Dietary
Fibre 3.5 g; Cholesterol 34 mg; 1980 kJ (475 Cal)

Ma por tofu

PREPARATION TIME: 15 MINUTES + 10 MINUTES MARINATING | TOTAL COOKING TIME: 15 MINUTES | SERVES 4

3 teaspoons cornflour (cornstarch)
2 teaspoons soy sauce
1 teaspoon oyster sauce
1 garlic clove, finely chopped
250 g (9 oz) minced (ground) pork
1 tablespoon oil
3 teaspoons red bean chilli paste
3 teaspoons preserved bean curd
750 g (1 lb 10 oz) firm tofu, drained, cubed
2 spring onions (scallions), sliced, plus extra
    shredded spring onion, to garnish
3 teaspoons oyster sauce, extra
2 teaspoons soy sauce, extra
1½ teaspoons sugar
finely sliced red capsicum (pepper), to garnish

1   Put the cornflour, soy and oyster sauces and the garlic in a bowl and mix well. Add the minced pork, toss to coat and leave for 10 minutes.

2   Heat a wok until very hot, add the oil and swirl to coat the side of the wok. Add the minced pork and stir-fry for 5 minutes, or until browned. Add the chilli paste and bean curd, and cook for 2 minutes, or until fragrant.

3   Add the remaining ingredients and stir-fry for 3–5 minutes, or until the tofu is heated through. Serve immediately, garnished with extra spring onion and capsicum.

NUTRITION PER SERVE
Protein 26 g; Fat 12 g; Carbohydrate 5 g; Dietary
Fibre 0 g; Cholesterol 30 mg; 1092 kJ (260 Cal)

Add the minced pork to the cornflour, soy sauce, oyster sauce and garlic.

Stir-fry the pork mixture until it is browned, then add the chilli paste and bean curd.

Phad thai

PREPARATION TIME: 25 MINUTES I TOTAL COOKING TIME: 10–15 MINUTES I SERVES 4

250 g (9 oz) thick rice stick noodles
2 tablespoons oil
3 garlic cloves, chopped
2 teaspoons chopped red chillies
150 g (5½ oz) pork, thinly sliced
100 g (3½ oz) raw prawns (shrimp), peeled,
    deveined and chopped
½ bunch garlic chives, snipped
2 tablespoons fish sauce
2 tablespoons lime juice
2 teaspoons soft brown sugar
2 eggs, beaten
90 g (3¼ oz/1 cup) bean sprouts
coriander (cilantro) sprigs
3 tablespoons chopped roasted peanuts
crisp-fried onion, soft brown sugar and extra
    chopped peanuts, to serve

1 Soak the rice stick noodles in warm water for 10 minutes, or until they are soft. Drain and set aside. Heat the wok until very hot, then add the oil and swirl to coat the side. When the oil is very hot, add the garlic, chilli and pork and stir-fry for 2 minutes.

2 Add the prawns and stir-fry for 3 minutes. Add the garlic chives and drained noodles to the wok; cover and cook for another minute.

3 Add the fish sauce, lime juice, sugar and eggs to the wok. Toss well until heated through.

4 Serve immediately, sprinkled with the bean sprouts, fresh coriander sprigs and chopped peanuts. Phad thai is traditionally served with crisp-fried onion, soft brown sugar and more chopped peanuts on the side.

NUTRITION PER SERVE
Protein 20 g; Fat 17 g; Carbohydrate 20 g; Dietary Fibre 2 g; Cholesterol 145 mg; 1334 kJ (320 Cal)

After stir-frying the pork for 2 minutes, stir in the chopped prawns.

Use two wooden spoons or a pair of tongs to toss the stir-fry.

Pork with snake beans

PREPARATION TIME: 15 MINUTES | TOTAL COOKING TIME: 20 MINUTES | SERVES 4

oil, for cooking
400 g (14 oz) pork fillet, thickly sliced
2 onions, thinly sliced
150 g (5½ oz) snake beans, diagonally sliced
3 garlic cloves, finely chopped
1 tablespoon finely chopped fresh ginger
1 red capsicum (pepper), thinly sliced
6 spring onions (scallions), diagonally sliced,
    plus extra shredded, to garnish
2 tablespoons sweet chilli sauce

1 Heat the wok until very hot, add 2 teaspoons of the oil and swirl it around to coat the side. Stir-fry the pork in two batches over high heat for 3–4 minutes, or until it is just cooked. Remove all the pork from the wok.

2 Heat 1 tablespoon of the oil over medium heat and add the sliced onion. Cook for 3–4 minutes. Add the sliced snake beans and cook for 2–3 minutes. Add the garlic, ginger, capsicum and spring onion, and toss well. Increase the heat and cook for 3–4 minutes.

3 Return the pork to the wok, add the sweet chilli sauce and toss well. Remove from the heat and season with salt and pepper. Serve immediately, garnished with shredded spring onion.

NUTRITION PER SERVE
Protein 25 g; Fat 12 g; Carbohydrate 8 g; Dietary Fibre 4 g; Cholesterol 50 mg; 1005 kJ (240 Cal)

Top and tail the snake beans, then cut them into diagonal slices.

Chiang Mai noodles

PREPARATION TIME: 20 MINUTES | TOTAL COOKING TIME: 15 MINUTES | SERVES 4

500 g (1 lb 2 oz) fresh egg noodles
1 tablespoon oil
3 Asian or French shallots (eschalots),
  chopped
6 garlic cloves, chopped
2 teaspoons finely chopped red chillies
1–2 tablespoons red curry paste, to taste
350 g (12 oz) lean pork, thinly sliced
1 carrot, cut into matchsticks
2 tablespoons fish sauce
2 teaspoons soft brown sugar
3 spring onions (scallions), finely sliced
1 medium handful coriander (cilantro)
  leaves
nam prik sauce, for serving (see page 248)

1   Cook the noodles in a wok or large pan of rapidly boiling water for 2–3 minutes, or until they are just tender. Drain and keep warm. Heat the oil in a wok until it is very hot. Add the shallots, garlic, chilli and curry paste and stir-fry for 2 minutes, or until fragrant. Add the pork in two batches and cook for 3 minutes, or until the meat changes colour.

2   Return all the meat to the wok. Add the carrot, fish sauce and brown sugar and bring to the boil. Add the noodles and spring onion and toss well. Top with coriander leaves and serve immediately with nam prik sauce.

NUTRITION PER SERVE
Protein 17 g; Fat 7.5 g; Carbohydrate 92 g; Dietary
Fibre 5 g; Cholesterol 23 mg; 2122 kJ (501 Cal)

Cook the noodles in a wok or pan of rapidly boiling water until just tender.

Return all the meat to the wok. Add the carrot, fish sauce and brown sugar.

Fried rice noodles

PREPARATION TIME: 30 MINUTES | TOTAL COOKING TIME: 15 MINUTES | SERVES 4

2 Chinese dried pork sausages (see NOTE)

2 tablespoons oil

2 garlic cloves, finely chopped

1 onion, finely chopped

3 red chillies, seeded and chopped

250 g (9 oz) Chinese barbecued pork, finely chopped

200 g (7 oz) raw prawns (shrimp), peeled and deveined

500 g (1 lb 2 oz) fresh thick rice noodles, gently separated

150 g (5½ oz/1 bunch) garlic chives, cut into 3 cm (1¼ inch) pieces

2 tablespoons kecap manis (see NOTE, page 18)

3 eggs, lightly beaten

1 tablespoon rice vinegar

100 g (3½ oz) bean sprouts, plus extra, to garnish

NUTRITION PER SERVE
Protein 47 g; Fat 17 g; Carbohydrate 30 g; Dietary Fibre 3 g; Cholesterol 285 mg; 1996 kJ (470 Cal)

1 Diagonally slice the dried pork sausages into paper-thin slices. Heat the oil in a large wok. Fry the sausage, tossing regularly, until golden and very crisp. Using a slotted spoon, remove from the wok and leave to drain on paper towels.

2 Reheat the oil in the wok, add the garlic, onion, chilli and pork and stir-fry for 2 minutes. Add the prawns and toss constantly, until the prawns change colour.

3 Add the noodles, chives and kecap manis and toss. Cook for 1 minute, or until the noodles begin to soften. Pour the combined eggs and vinegar over the top of the noodles and toss for 1 minute. Be careful not to overcook the noodles, or let the egg-coated noodles burn on the base of the wok. Toss in the bean sprouts.

4 Arrange on a large serving platter, scatter the sausage over the top and toss a little to mix a few slices among the noodles. Serve immediately, garnished with extra bean sprouts.

NOTE: *Chinese pork sausages (lup chiang) must always be cooked before eating.*

Remove the crisp Chinese sausage slices from the wok and drain on paper towels.

Pour the combined eggs and vinegar over the top of the noodles and toss.

Thai red pork curry with corn and peas

PREPARATION TIME: 15 MINUTES I TOTAL COOKING TIME: 25 MINUTES I SERVES 4

1 tablespoon oil

1–2 tablespoons red curry paste, to taste

500 g (1 lb 2 oz) lean pork, diced

250 ml (9 fl oz/1 cup) coconut milk

200 g (7 oz/1 cup) fresh corn kernels or
150 g (5½ oz) baby corn spears

90 g (3¼ oz/½ cup) fresh peas

1 tablespoon fish sauce

2 teaspoons soft brown sugar

2 teaspoons finely grated lime zest

1 very large handful Thai basil, shredded

1   Heat the oil in a wok and swirl to coat the sides. Add the curry paste and stir-fry for 1 minute. Add the pork and stir-fry until lightly browned.

2   Add the coconut milk and 250 ml (9 fl oz/ 1 cup) water and bring to the boil. Simmer for 15 minutes.

3   Add the corn and peas to the wok and cook for 5 minutes. Add the fish sauce, brown sugar, lime zest and basil leaves and toss well.

Add the diced pork to the wok and toss the meat until it turns light brown.

Simmer the mixture in the wok for 15 minutes so that the sauce reduces and thickens.

NUTRITION PER SERVE
Protein 30 g; Fat 20 g; Carbohydrate 13 g; Dietary Fibre 3.5 g; Cholesterol 62 mg; 1535 kJ (367 Cal)

Coriander pork with fresh pineapple

PREPARATION TIME: 25 MINUTES | TOTAL COOKING TIME: 10–12 MINUTES | SERVES 4

400 g (14 oz) pork loin or fillet
¼ pineapple
1 tablespoon oil
4 garlic cloves, chopped
4 spring onions (scallions), chopped
1 tablespoon fish sauce
1 tablespoon lime juice
1 very large handful coriander (cilantro) leaves
3 tablespoons chopped mint

1 Cut the pork into thin slices, using a very sharp knife (see HINT).

2 Trim the skin from the pineapple and cut the flesh into small bite-sized pieces. Heat the oil in a wok, add the garlic and spring onion and cook for 1 minute. Remove from the wok.

3 Heat the wok to very hot, add the pork in two or three batches and stir-fry each batch for 3 minutes, or until the meat is just cooked. Return the meat, garlic and spring onion to the wok and then add the pineapple pieces, fish sauce and lime juice. Toss well. Just before serving, sprinkle with the coriander leaves and chopped mint and then toss together lightly.

HINT: *To make the meat easier to slice, freeze it until it is firm and slice thinly while still frozen.*

NUTRITION PER SERVE
Protein 24 g; Fat 7 g; Carbohydrate 7 g; Dietary Fibre 2 g; Cholesterol 50 mg; 762 kJ (182 Cal)

Buy pork loin or fillet and use a sharp knife to cut it into thin slices.

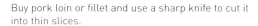

Slice the skin from the pineapple and cut the flesh into small, bite-sized pieces.

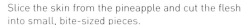

Stir-fry each batch of pork for 3 minutes, or until just cooked.

Savoury rice and eggs

PREPARATION TIME: 20 MINUTES | TOTAL COOKING TIME: 12 MINUTES | SERVES 4

2 tablespoons ghee (see HINT) or oil

1 onion, finely chopped

½ red capsicum (pepper), finely chopped, plus extra finely sliced capsicum, to garnish

10 spring onions (scallions), thinly sliced, plus extra finely shredded spring onion, to garnish

2–3 small red chillies, seeded and finely chopped

2–3 garlic cloves, finely chopped

1 tablespoon grated fresh ginger

125 g (4½ oz) Chinese barbecued pork, finely chopped

6 eggs, lightly beaten

740 g (1 lb 10 oz/4 cups) cold cooked jasmine rice

1 teaspoon soy sauce

2 large handfuls coriander (cilantro), chopped

crisp-fried onion, to garnish

1 Heat the wok until very hot, add the ghee and swirl it around to coat the side. Stir-fry the onion, capsicum, spring onion, chilli, garlic and ginger over medium–high heat for 2–3 minutes, or until the vegetables are cooked but not brown. Add the barbecue pork and toss to combine.

2 Reduce the heat, then pour in the beaten eggs. Season well with salt and pepper. Gently stir the egg mixture until it is creamy and almost set. Add the rice and gently stir-fry to incorporate all the ingredients and heat the mixture through.

3 Sprinkle with the soy sauce and stir in the coriander. Serve the savoury rice immediately, topped with sliced capsicum, shredded spring onion and crisp-fried onion.

HINT: *Ghee is a form of clarified butter. It is the main type of fat used in Indian cooking and is available in most supermarkets.*

NUTRITION PER SERVE
Protein 15 g; Fat 20 g; Carbohydrate 60 g; Dietary Fibre 3.5 g; Cholesterol 295 mg; 2105 kJ (500 Cal)

Cut the Chinese barbecued pork into slices, then chop it finely.

Add the barbecued pork to the onion mixture and toss to combine.

Add the egg, season well and stir gently until the mixture is creamy.

Fried rice with coriander and basil

PREPARATION TIME: 20 MINUTES I TOTAL COOKING TIME: 20 MINUTES I SERVES 4

2 tablespoons oil

2.5 cm (1 inch) piece pork fat, chopped

4 garlic cloves, chopped

5 cm (2 inch) piece fresh ginger, grated

2 teaspoons chopped red chillies

2 boneless, skinless chicken thighs, diced

100 g (3½ oz) pork loin, diced

500 g (1 lb 2 oz/2¾ cups) cold cooked
    jasmine rice

1 tablespoon fish sauce

2 teaspoons soy sauce

2 spring onions (scallions), chopped

1 very large handful Thai basil leaves, chopped

1 very large handful coriander (cilantro)
    leaves, chopped, plus some to garnish

1   Heat the oil in a wok. When the oil is very hot, add the pork fat, garlic, ginger and chilli and stir-fry for 2 minutes.

2   Add the diced chicken and pork to the wok and stir-fry for 3 minutes, or until the meat changes colour. Add the rice to the wok and toss well using two wooden spoons, breaking up any lumps. When the rice has warmed, add the sauces and toss through with the spring onions, Thai basil and coriander. Serve immediately.

NUTRITION PER SERVE
Protein 25 g; Fat 40 g; Carbohydrate 45 g; Dietary Fibre 5 g; Cholesterol 46 mg; 2752 kJ (657 Cal)

Buy pork loin and then dice it with a sharp knife.

Add the pork fat, garlic, ginger and chillies to the wok and stir with a wooden spoon.

Add the cold cooked rice to the wok and toss well, breaking up any lumps.

Pork and peanut dip

PREPARATION TIME: 25 MINUTES | TOTAL COOKING TIME: 20 MINUTES | SERVES 6–8

1 teaspoon green peppercorns
1 tablespoon oil
2 coriander (cilantro) roots, very
    finely chopped
2 garlic cloves, finely chopped
150 g (5½ oz) minced (ground) pork
125 ml (4 fl oz/½ cup) coconut milk
3 tablespoons crunchy peanut butter
1 tablespoon fish sauce
2 teaspoons soft brown sugar
coriander (cilantro) leaves, to garnish
roasted chopped unsalted peanuts
chilli sauce
vegetable crudités or savoury biscuits, to serve

1   Finely crush the peppercorns, using the flat side of the blade of a knife. Heat the oil in a wok.

2   Add the peppercorns, coriander roots and garlic to the wok and stir for 30 seconds over medium heat. Add the minced pork and stir-fry for 5 minutes, breaking up any lumps of meat with a fork or wooden spoon. Add the coconut milk, peanut butter and 125 ml (4 fl oz/½ cup) water. Bring to the boil, stirring. Reduce the heat and allow to simmer for 10 minutes.

3   Stir in the fish sauce and brown sugar. Pour into a serving bowl and sprinkle with the coriander and peanuts. Drizzle with chilli sauce. Serve warm or at room temperature, with crudités and savoury biscuits for dipping.

Finely crush the green peppercorns, using the flat side of the blade of a knife.

Add the minced pork to the wok after cooking the peppercorns, coriander and garlic.

NUTRITION PER SERVE (8)
Protein 8 g; Fat 12 g; Carbohydrate 3 g; Dietary Fibre 1.5 g; Cholesterol 9 mg; 625 kJ (150 Cal)

Lamb

Warm lamb salad

PREPARATION TIME: 15 MINUTES + 3 HOURS REFRIGERATION | TOTAL COOKING TIME: 15 MINUTES | SERVES 4–6

2 tablespoons red curry paste
1 very large handful coriander (cilantro)
    leaves, chopped
1 tablespoon finely grated fresh ginger
3–4 tablespoons peanut oil
750 g (1 lb 10 oz) lamb fillets, thinly sliced
200 g (7 oz) snow peas (mangetouts)
600 g (1 lb 5 oz) packet thick fresh
    rice noodles
1 red capsicum (pepper), thinly sliced
1 Lebanese (short) cucumber, thinly sliced
6 spring onions (scallions), thinly sliced

MINT DRESSING
1½ tablespoons peanut oil
60 ml (2 fl oz/¼ cup) lime juice
2 tablespoons soft brown sugar
3 teaspoons fish sauce
3 teaspoons soy sauce
1 very large handful mint leaves, chopped
1 garlic clove, crushed

1 Combine the curry paste, coriander, ginger and 2 tablespoons peanut oil in a bowl. Add the lamb and coat well. Cover and refrigerate for 2–3 hours.

2 Steam or boil the snow peas until just tender, refresh under cold water and drain.

3 Cover the noodles with boiling water. Leave for 5 minutes, or until tender, and drain.

4 To make the dressing, put all the ingredients in a screw-top jar and shake well.

5 Heat a wok until very hot, add 1 tablespoon peanut oil and swirl to coat. Add half the lamb and stir-fry for 5 minutes, or until tender. Repeat with the remaining lamb, using more oil if needed.

6 Place the lamb, snow peas, noodles, capsicum, cucumber and spring onion in a large bowl, drizzle with the dressing and toss before serving.

NUTRITION PER SERVE (6)
Protein 32 g; Fat 20 g; Carbohydrate 33 g; Dietary Fibre 3 g; Cholesterol 83 mg; 1850 kJ (442 Cal)

Mix together the curry paste, coriander, ginger and 2 tablespoons peanut oil.

Leave the thick fresh rice noodles in boiling water until they are tender, then drain.

Put all the dressing ingredients in a screw-top jar and shake them well to mix.

Mongolian lamb

PREPARATION TIME: 15 MINUTES I TOTAL COOKING TIME: 12 MINUTES I SERVES 4

oil, for cooking
500 g (1 lb 2 oz) lamb backstrap (loin fillet),
    thinly sliced
2 garlic cloves, crushed
4 spring onions (scallions), thickly sliced
2 tablespoons soy sauce
80 ml (2½ fl oz/⅓ cup) dry sherry
2 tablespoons sweet chilli sauce
2 teaspoons sesame seeds, toasted

1   Heat the wok until very hot, add
1 tablespoon of the oil and swirl it around to
coat the side of the wok. Stir-fry the lamb strips
in batches over high heat, adding more oil
whenever necessary. Remove all the lamb from
the wok.

2   Reheat the wok, add 1 tablespoon of oil and
stir-fry the garlic and spring onion for 2 minutes.
Remove from the wok and set aside. Add the soy
sauce, sherry and sweet chilli sauce to the wok.
Bring to the boil, reduce the heat and simmer for
3–4 minutes, or until the sauce thickens slightly.

3   Return the meat, with any juices, and the
spring onion to the wok, and toss to coat with
the sauce. Serve sprinkled with the toasted
sesame seeds.

NUTRITION PER SERVE
Protein 30 g; Fat 20 g; Carbohydrate 7 g; Dietary
Fibre 1.5 g; Cholesterol 80 mg; 1445 kJ (345 Cal)

Slice the lamb backstrap into thin strips with a sharp knife.

Stir-fry the lamb strips in batches over high heat so that they fry rather than stew.

Add the soy sauce, sherry and sweet chilli sauce to the wok and bring to the boil.

Satay lamb

PREPARATION TIME: 20 MINUTES | TOTAL COOKING TIME: 15 MINUTES | SERVES 4–6

oil, for cooking
500 g (1 lb 2 oz) lamb fillet, thinly sliced
1 onion, chopped
2 garlic cloves, crushed
2 teaspoons grated fresh ginger
1–2 red chillies, seeded and finely chopped
1 teaspoon ground cumin
1 teaspoon ground coriander
125 g (4½ oz/½ cup) crunchy peanut butter
1 tablespoon soy sauce
2 tablespoons lemon juice
125 ml (4 fl oz/½ cup) coconut cream
finely sliced red capsicum (pepper), to garnish

1 Heat the wok until very hot, add
1 tablespoon oil and swirl it around to coat the
side. Stir-fry the lamb in batches over high heat
until it is well browned and cooked, adding
more oil when necessary. Remove the lamb from
the wok and set aside.

2 Reheat the wok, add 1 tablespoon of the
oil and stir-fry the onion over medium heat for
2–3 minutes, or until soft and transparent. Stir
in the garlic, ginger, chilli, cumin and coriander,
and cook for 1 minute.

3 Stir in the peanut butter, soy sauce, lemon
juice, coconut cream and 125 ml (4 fl oz/½ cup)
water. Slowly bring to the boil. Return the lamb
to the wok and stir until heated through. Serve
garnished with sliced capsicum.

NUTRITION PER SERVE (6)
Protein 25 g; Fat 25 g; Carbohydrate 5 g; Dietary
Fibre 3 g; Cholesterol 55 mg; 1390 kJ (330 Cal)

Stir-fry the onion over medium heat until it is soft
and transparent.

Add the garlic, ginger, chilli, cumin and coriander
to the onion.

Garlic lamb with wilted mushrooms and noodles

PREPARATION TIME: 30 MINUTES | TOTAL COOKING TIME: 20 MINUTES | SERVES 4

350 g (12 oz) lamb fillet, sliced diagonally
8 Asian shallots (eschalots), very thinly sliced
4 garlic cloves, finely chopped
1½ tablespoons oil
1 teaspoon soft brown sugar
300 g (10½ oz) fresh egg noodles
oil, extra, for cooking
200 g (7 oz) button mushrooms, sliced
150 g (5½ oz) small oyster mushrooms
2 tablespoons teriyaki sauce
75 g (2½ oz) fresh garlic chives, cut into
　short pieces

NUTRITION PER SERVE
Protein 30 g; Fat 20 g; Carbohydrate 40 g; Dietary
Fibre 3 g; Cholesterol 60 mg; 1920 kJ (460 Cal)

1 Combine the lamb, shallots, garlic, oil, brown sugar, 1 teaspoon salt and 1 teaspoon freshly ground black pepper in a bowl. Mix well.

2 Cook the noodles in boiling salted water for 3 minutes, or until just tender. Rinse in cold water.

3 Heat the wok until very hot, add 1 tablespoon of oil and swirl it around to coat the side. Stir-fry the lamb in three batches until browned, adding a little more oil when needed. Remove all the meat from the wok.

4 Add the button mushrooms to the wok with 2 teaspoons of water and stir-fry for 1 minute. Add the oyster mushrooms and teriyaki sauce and toss well. Cover and steam for about 10 seconds.

5 Return all the lamb and any juices to the wok with the noodles and chives. Toss well to heat through. Serve immediately.

Trim any fat from the lamb with a sharp knife and slice into diagonal strips.

Asian shallots look rather like large cloves of garlic with a pink papery skin.

Stir-fry the marinated lamb in batches, tossing constantly until it is well browned.

Sweet mustard lamb

PREPARATION TIME: 15 MINUTES | TOTAL COOKING TIME: 15 MINUTES | SERVES 4

oil, for cooking
500 g (1 lb 2 oz) lamb fillet, cut into thin strips
2 garlic cloves, crushed
250 g (9 oz) snow peas (mangetouts)
1 onion, cut into large wedges
20 g (¾ oz) salted butter
60 g (2¼ oz/¼ cup) wholegrain mustard
1 tablespoon honey
125 ml (4 fl oz/½ cup) pouring
    (whipping) cream
2 tablespoons brandy, optional

1 Heat the wok until very hot, add
1 tablespoon of the oil and swirl it around to coat
the side. Stir-fry the lamb strips in batches over
high heat. Remove from the wok and set aside.

2 Heat 1 tablespoon of the oil in the wok
and add the crushed garlic, snow peas and
onion wedges. Stir-fry over medium heat for
3–4 minutes, or until the onion softens slightly.
Remove from the wok and keep warm.

3 Reduce the heat and add the butter, mustard,
honey, cream and brandy. Simmer gently for
3–4 minutes. Return the meat and vegetables to
the wok and stir until they are heated through
and combined with the sauce.

NUTRITION PER SERVE
Protein 30 g; Fat 30 g; Carbohydrate 15 g; Dietary
Fibre 4 g; Cholesterol 140 mg; 2030 kJ (485 Cal)

Remove any fat or sinew from the lamb fillet and cut the lamb into thin strips.

Stir-fry the lamb slices in batches over high heat until the meat browns.

Heat the oil and add the garlic, snow peas and onion wedges.

Indian lamb and spinach

PREPARATION TIME: 20 MINUTES + AT LEAST 2 HOURS MARINATING | TOTAL COOKING TIME: 20 MINUTES | SERVES 4

2 garlic cloves, finely chopped
1 tablespoon finely chopped fresh ginger
1 tablespoon ground cumin
1 tablespoon ground coriander
1 teaspoon ground cinnamon
½ teaspoon ground allspice
60 ml (2 fl oz/¼ cup) oil
600 g (1 lb 5 oz) lamb fillet, sliced diagonally
oil, extra, for cooking
2 onions, thinly sliced
500 g (1 lb 2 oz) English spinach, shredded
1 tablespoon lime juice
2 tablespoons toasted pine nuts

1 Combine the garlic, ginger, ½ teaspoon salt, spices and oil in a shallow glass or ceramic bowl. Add the sliced lamb and mix until well combined. Cover and refrigerate for at least 2 hours.

2 Heat the wok until very hot, and stir-fry the lamb in three batches over high heat for 2–3 minutes, or until the lamb is golden brown and just cooked. Remove the lamb from the wok and cover to keep warm.

3 Reheat the wok and add 1 tablespoon of the oil. Stir-fry the sliced onion over medium–high heat for 2–3 minutes, or until slightly softened. Add the spinach, cover and steam for 1–2 minutes, or until the spinach has just wilted. Return all the lamb and juices to the wok along with the lime juice and toasted pine nuts. Toss until thoroughly combined and season well with salt and pepper. Serve immediately.

NUTRITION PER SERVE
Protein 40 g; Fat 25 g; Carbohydrate 5 g; Dietary Fibre 5 g; Cholesterol 100 mg; 1735 kJ (415 Cal)

Toast the pine nuts by dry-frying them in the wok before you start.

Stir-fry the marinated lamb in batches so that it fries rather than stews.

Spicy lamb and eggplant

PREPARATION TIME: 15 MINUTES | TOTAL COOKING TIME: 20 MINUTES | SERVES 4

oil, for cooking
1 onion, finely chopped
500 g (1 lb 2 oz) eggplant (aubergine), peeled
    and cut into batons
600 g (1 lb 5 oz) lamb fillet, thinly sliced
    diagonally
2 garlic cloves, finely chopped
1 small red chilli, seeded and finely chopped
1 tablespoon ground cumin
1 tablespoon ground coriander
2 teaspoons ground turmeric
1 teaspoon ground cinnamon
250 ml (9 fl oz/1 cup) thick coconut cream
1 tablespoon mint leaves
2 tablespoons parsley leaves
lemon wedges, to serve

1 Heat the wok until very hot, add 2 teaspoons of the oil and swirl it around to coat the side. Stir-fry the onion until soft and golden. Remove from the wok and set aside.

2 Add 1 tablespoon of the oil to the wok and cook the eggplant in two batches over high heat until golden brown and cooked through. Remove and drain on paper towels.

3 Reheat the wok and add 2 teaspoons of the oil. Stir-fry the lamb in two batches over high heat until browned and just cooked.

4 Return all the lamb to the wok with the onion and eggplant. Add the garlic, chilli and spices and cook for 1 minute. Pour in the coconut cream and bring to the boil.

5 Stir in the fresh herbs and season with salt and pepper. Serve with the lemon wedges.

NUTRITION PER SERVE
Protein 35 g; Fat 30 g; Carbohydrate 7 g; Dietary Fibre 5 g; Cholesterol 100 mg; 1775 kJ (425 Cal)

Peel the eggplant, remove the ends and cut the eggplant into batons.

Cook the eggplant in the oil until it has turned golden brown.

Return the lamb, onion and eggplant to the wok and add the garlic, chilli and spices.

Peppered lamb and asparagus

PREPARATION TIME: 35 MINUTES + 20 MINUTES MARINATING | TOTAL COOKING TIME: 20 MINUTES | SERVES 4

400 g (14 oz) lamb fillets
2 teaspoons green peppercorns,
    finely chopped
3 garlic cloves, finely chopped
1 tablespoon vegetable oil
1 onion, cut into small wedges
80 ml (2½ fl oz/⅓ cup) dry sherry
1 green capsicum (pepper), cut into strips
½ teaspoon sugar
16 small asparagus spears, chopped, tough
    ends discarded
200 g (7 oz) broccoli florets
2 tablespoons oyster sauce
garlic chives, snipped, to garnish

1   Trim away any sinew from the lamb and cut
the lamb into bite-sized pieces. Combine in a
bowl with the green peppercorns, garlic and oil,
then toss well and set aside for 20 minutes.

2   Heat a wok over high heat until slightly
smoking. Add the lamb in batches and stir-fry
until browned. Remove, cover and keep warm.

3   Reheat the wok and stir-fry the onion and
2 teaspoons of the sherry for 1 minute. Add the
capsicum, sugar and a large pinch of salt. Cover
and steam for 2 minutes. Add the asparagus,
broccoli and the remaining sherry and stir-fry for
1 minute. Cover and steam for 3 minutes, or until
the vegetables are just tender. Return the lamb to
the wok, add the oyster sauce and stir well. Top
with the chives.

Stir-fry the lamb over high heat until brown and
just cooked.

Add the asparagus and broccoli to the capsicum
and onion.

NUTRITION PER SERVE
Protein 25 g; Fat 12 g; Carbohydrate 8 g; Dietary
Fibre 4 g; Cholesterol 65 mg; 1100 kJ (265 Cal)

Chilli lamb and cashews

PREPARATION TIME: 10 MINUTES | TOTAL COOKING TIME: 10 MINUTES | SERVES 4

750 g (1 lb 10 oz) lamb fillets
4 tablespoons peanut oil
150 g (5½ oz/1 cup) cashew nuts
1 large onion, cut into wedges
200 g (7 oz) snow peas (mangetouts)
225 g (8 oz) sliced bamboo shoots
2 tablespoons chilli sauce
1 tablespoon soy sauce

1 Trim the meat of any fat and sinew and then cut across the grain evenly into thin slices. Heat 2 tablespoons of the oil in a wok, swirling gently to coat the side. Stir-fry the lamb in small batches over high heat until browned but not cooked through. Remove from the wok and drain on paper towels.

2 Heat 1 tablespoon oil in the wok and fry the cashews until golden brown. Remove with a slotted spoon and drain on paper towels.

3 Heat the remaining oil in the wok and stir-fry the onion and snow peas for 2 minutes. Add the bamboo shoots and stir-fry for 1 minute. Return the meat to the wok with the cashews and chilli and soy sauces. Stir-fry over high heat until the meat is cooked and the sauce is hot. Serve immediately.

NUTRITION PER SERVE
Protein 52 g; Fat 45 g; Carbohydrate 15 g; Dietary Fibre 7 g; Cholesterol 124 mg; 2784 kJ (665 Cal)

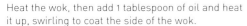
Heat the wok, then add 1 tablespoon of oil and heat it up, swirling to coat the side of the wok.

Stir-fry the cashews until they are golden brown, then remove with a slotted spoon.

Return the browned meat to the wok with the fried cashew nuts.

Lamb with mixed greens

PREPARATION TIME: 10 MINUTES | TOTAL COOKING TIME: 15 MINUTES | SERVES 4

500 g (1 lb 2 oz) lamb fillets, cut into strips
    about 2.5 cm (1 inch) wide
1 egg white, lightly beaten
cornflour (cornstarch), for coating
2–3 tablespoons oil
2.5 cm (1 inch) piece fresh ginger,
    thinly sliced
2 garlic cloves, crushed
2 tablespoons soy sauce
2 leeks, finely sliced
250 g (9 oz) baby English spinach
    leaves, torn
1 small bunch bok choy (pak choy), cut into
    short lengths
115 g (4 oz/¾ cup) frozen peas
1 teaspoon sugar
3 tablespoons chicken stock
dash of chilli sauce

1 Season the strips of lamb with salt and pepper, dip in the egg white and dust with cornflour.

2 Heat half the oil in a wok and add the ginger, garlic and soy sauce. Stir-fry over high heat for 30 seconds. Add the lamb and stir-fry for 1 minute, or until browned. Reduce the heat, cover and cook for 3 minutes. Remove the lamb from the wok.

3 Heat the remaining oil in the wok and add the leek. Stir-fry over high heat for 3 minutes, or until the leek has softened.

4 Add the spinach, bok choy and frozen peas to the wok and stir-fry for 1 minute. Reduce the heat, cover the wok and steam the vegetables for 2 minutes. Combine the sugar, stock and chilli sauce and add to the wok. Add the lamb and stir well. Stir-fry for 2 minutes, or until the lamb and vegetables are just tender.

NUTRITION PER SERVE
Protein 35 g; Fat 30 g; Carbohydrate 7 g; Dietary Fibre 5 g; Cholesterol 100 mg; 1775 kJ (425 Cal)

Season the meat with salt and pepper, then dip in the egg white and cornflour.

Add the spinach, bok choy and frozen peas to the wok and stir-fry for 1 minute.

Chicken
and duck

Goan-style chicken with sultanas and almonds

PREPARATION TIME: 20 MINUTES I TOTAL COOKING TIME: 20 MINUTES I SERVES 3–4

2 teaspoons ground cumin

2 teaspoons ground coriander

1 teaspoon ground cinnamon

½ teaspoon cayenne pepper

½ teaspoon ground cardamom

oil, for cooking

1 large onion, cut into thin wedges

2 garlic cloves, finely chopped

500 g (1 lb 2 oz) boneless, skinless chicken
    breasts, cubed

2 teaspoons finely grated orange zest

2 tablespoons orange juice

2 tablespoons sultanas

1 teaspoon soft brown sugar

60 g (2¼ oz/¼ cup) thick plain yoghurt

40 g (1½ oz/⅓ cup) slivered almonds, toasted

1   Dry-fry the spices in a wok over low heat for about 1 minute, or until fragrant, stirring constantly.

2   Add 1 tablespoon oil and stir-fry the onion wedges and garlic over high heat for 3 minutes. Remove from the wok.

3   Reheat the wok, add 1 tablespoon of the oil and stir-fry the chicken in two batches until it is golden and just cooked. Return all the chicken to the wok with the onion mixture, orange zest, juice, sultanas and sugar. Cook for 1 minute, tossing, until most of the juice evaporates.

4   Stir in the yoghurt and reheat gently, without boiling, or the yoghurt will separate. Season well with salt and pepper. Serve garnished with the toasted almonds.

HINT: *Yoghurt separates easily when it is heated, due to its acid balance. Yoghurt also separates when shaken, whipped or stirred too much.*

NUTRITION PER SERVE (4)
Protein 30 g; Fat 20 g; Carbohydrate 15 g; Dietary Fibre 2.5 g; Cholesterol 65 mg; 1500 kJ (360 Cal)

Toast the almonds by dry-frying them in the wok until golden brown.

Dry-dry the spices over low heat until they have become fragrant.

Stir-fry the onion and garlic until they are coated in the spices.

Duck, orange and bok choy

PREPARATION TIME: 25 MINUTES | COOKING TIME: 15 MINUTES | SERVES 4

1 Chinese barbecued duck (about 1 kg/
  2 lb 4 oz), boned (ask the vendor to bone
  it for you)
1 tablespoon oil
1 onion, sliced
2 garlic cloves, crushed
2 teaspoons grated fresh ginger
1 tablespoon orange zest
170 ml (5½ fl oz/⅔ cup) orange juice
60 ml (2 fl oz/¼ cup) chicken stock
2 teaspoons soft brown sugar
2 teaspoons cornflour (cornstarch)
1.5 kg (3 lb 5 oz) baby bok choy (pak choy),
  leaves separated
1 orange, segmented

1 Cut the duck meat into pieces. Reserve and thinly slice some crisp skin for garnish. Heat the wok until very hot, add the oil and swirl it around to coat the side. Stir-fry the onion for 3 minutes, or until tender. Stir in the garlic and ginger for 1–2 minutes. Pour in the combined orange zest, juice, stock and sugar. Bring to the boil.

2 Mix the cornflour with a little water to form a paste. Pour into the wok, stirring until the mixture boils and thickens. Place the duck pieces in the sauce and simmer for 1–2 minutes, or until heated through. Remove from the wok and keep warm.

3 Place the bok choy in the wok with 2 tablespoons water. Cover and steam until just wilted. Arrange on a serving plate, spoon the duck mixture over the top and garnish with the orange segments and the crisp duck skin.

Cut downwards to remove the zest and pith from the orange.

Segment the orange by slicing between the membrane and the flesh.

NUTRITION PER SERVE
Protein 9 g; Fat 40 g; Carbohydrate 25 g; Dietary
Fibre 3.5 g; Cholesterol 0 mg; 2975 kJ (710 Cal)

Vietnamese chicken with pineapple and cashews

PREPARATION TIME: 35 MINUTES | TOTAL COOKING TIME: 25 MINUTES | SERVES 4

90 g (3¼ oz/½ cup) raw cashew nuts

2 tablespoons oil

4 garlic cloves, finely chopped

1 large onion, cut in to large chunks

2 teaspoons chopped red chillies

350 g (12 oz) boneless, skinless chicken thighs, chopped

½ red capsicum (pepper), chopped

½ green capsicum (pepper), chopped

2 tablespoons oyster sauce

1 tablespoon fish sauce

1 teaspoon sugar

320 g (11¼ oz/2 cups) chopped fresh pineapple

3 spring onions (scallions), shredded

2 tablespoons shredded coconut, toasted

1 Roast the cashews on an oven tray for about 15 minutes in a moderate 180°C (350°F/Gas 4) oven, until deep golden. Allow to cool.

2 Heat the oil in a wok and stir-fry the garlic, onion and chilli over medium heat for 2 minutes; remove from the wok. Increase the heat to high and stir-fry the chicken and capsicum, in two batches, tossing until the chicken is light brown.

3 Return the onion and chilli to the wok, add the oyster sauce, fish sauce, sugar and pineapple and toss for 2 minutes to heat through. Toss the cashews through. Arrange on a serving plate and scatter the spring onion and coconut over the top. Serve immediately.

NUTRITION PER SERVE
Protein 25 g; Fat 24 g; Carbohydrate 18 g; Dietary Fibre 5 g; Cholesterol 44 mg; 1629 kJ (390 Cal)

Roast the cashews on an oven tray for 15 minutes, or until golden.

Stir-fry the chicken and capsicum until the chicken is light brown.

Warm curried chicken salad

PREPARATION TIME: 15 MINUTES + OVERNIGHT MARINATING | TOTAL COOKING TIME: 10 MINUTES | SERVES 4–6

3 tablespoons mild Indian curry paste
60 ml (2 fl oz/¼ cup) coconut milk
750 g (1 lb 10 oz) boneless, skinless chicken
   breasts, sliced
150 g (5½ oz) green beans, halved
2 tablespoons peanut oil
30 g (1 oz/⅓ cup) flaked almonds, toasted
1 red capsicum (pepper), sliced
250 g (9 oz) rocket (arugula)
100 g (3½ oz) fried egg noodles

LEMON DRESSING
80 ml (2½ fl oz/⅓ cup) olive oil
2 tablespoons lemon juice
2 garlic cloves, crushed
1 teaspoon soft brown sugar

1 Mix together the curry paste and coconut milk, add the chicken, toss to coat, cover and refrigerate overnight.

2 Cook the beans in boiling water for 30 seconds, or until just tender. Refresh under cold water. Drain.

3 Heat a wok until very hot, add half the oil and swirl to coat the side of the wok. Cook the chicken in two batches, for 5 minutes each batch, until browned, using the remaining oil for the second batch. Remove from the wok.

4 To make the dressing, place the ingredients in a screw-top jar and shake well.

5 Place the chicken, beans, almonds, capsicum, rocket and dressing in a large bowl and mix well. Stir in the noodles and serve.

NUTRITION PER SERVE (6)
Protein 32 g; Fat 29 g; Carbohydrate 6.5 g; Dietary Fibre 2.5 g; Cholesterol 72 mg; 1730 kJ (412 Cal)

Toast the flaked almonds on a baking tray in the oven or under a grill (broiler) before you start.

Cook the beans in boiling water for 30 seconds and then refresh in cold water.

Brown the chicken in two batches, using half the oil for each batch.

Duck and pineapple curry

PREPARATION TIME: 10 MINUTES | TOTAL COOKING TIME: 15 MINUTES | SERVES 4–6

1 tablespoon peanut oil

8 spring onions (scallions), cut into
short lengths

2 garlic cloves, crushed

1 tablespoon red curry paste

750 g (1 lb 10 oz) Chinese barbecued duck,
chopped into large bite-sized pieces
(see HINT)

400 ml (14 fl oz) coconut milk

450 g (1 lb) tin pineapple pieces in
syrup, drained

3 makrut (kaffir lime) leaves (see NOTE,
page 33)

1 very large handful coriander
(cilantro), chopped

2 tablespoons chopped mint

1 Heat a wok until very hot, add the oil and
swirl to coat. Add the spring onion, garlic and
curry paste, and stir-fry for 1 minute, or until the
paste is fragrant.

2 Add the remaining ingredients. Bring to
the boil, then reduce the heat and simmer for
10 minutes, or until the duck is heated through.

HINT: *You can ask the vendor to chop the duck.*

NUTRITION PER SERVE (6)
Protein 4 g; Fat 32 g; Carbohydrate 25 g; Dietary
Fibre 4.5 g; Cholesterol 10 mg; 1705 kJ (405 Cal)

Chop the barbecued duck into smaller pieces, or
ask for this to be done when you buy it.

Cook the spring onion, garlic and curry paste for
1 minute, or until the paste is fragrant.

Add the remaining ingredients to the wok and
simmer for 10 minutes.

Middle Eastern chicken

PREPARATION TIME: 10 MINUTES | TOTAL COOKING TIME: 20 MINUTES | SERVES 4

2 tablespoons oil
2 boneless, skinless chicken breasts,
　　thinly sliced
1 red onion, thinly sliced
310 g (11 oz) tin chickpeas, drained
75 g (2½ oz/½ cup) unsalted pistachio kernels
1 tomato, chopped
juice of 1 orange
1 medium handful flat-leaf (Italian) parsley,
　　finely chopped

1　Heat a wok over high heat, add half the oil and swirl to coat the side of the wok. Add the chicken in batches and stir-fry for 3–5 minutes, or until cooked. Remove from the wok and keep warm.

2　Add the remaining oil to the wok and stir-fry the onion for 2 minutes, then add the chickpeas, pistachio kernels and tomato. Stir-fry for 3–5 minutes, or until the chickpeas are warmed through.

3　Pour in the orange juice, return the chicken and its juices to the wok and stir-fry until half the juice has evaporated. Stir through the parsley. Season well and serve (couscous is the ideal accompaniment).

NUTRITION PER SERVE
Protein 37 g; Fat 25 g; Carbohydrate 17 g; Dietary
Fibre 6.5 g; Cholesterol 60 mg; 1785 kJ (425 Cal)

Stir-fry the chicken in batches so that the wok isn't overcrowded.

Stir-fry the onion for 2 minutes, then add the chickpeas, pistachio kernels and tomato.

Stir-fry until half the juice has evaporated, then add the parsley and seasoning.

Chicken chow mein

PREPARATION TIME: 25 MINUTES + 1 HOUR MARINATING | TOTAL COOKING TIME: 20 MINUTES | SERVES 4–6

500 g (1 lb 2 oz) boneless, skinless chicken
   thighs, cut into small cubes
1 tablespoon cornflour (cornstarch)
2 tablespoons soy sauce
1 tablespoon oyster sauce
2 teaspoons sugar
oil, for cooking
2 onions, thinly sliced
2 garlic cloves, finely chopped
1 tablespoon finely chopped fresh ginger
1 green capsicum (pepper), cubed
2 celery stalks, diagonally sliced
8 spring onions (scallions), cut into
   short pieces, plus extra finely shredded
   spring onion, to garnish
100 g (3½ oz) mushrooms, thinly sliced
80 g (2¾ oz/½ cup) water chestnuts,
   thinly sliced
2 teaspoons cornflour (cornstarch), extra
1 tablespoon Chinese rice wine
125 ml (4 fl oz/½ cup) chicken stock
1 tablespoon soy sauce, extra
90 g (3¼ oz) finely shredded Chinese
   cabbage
200 g (7 oz) fried egg noodles

1   In a glass or ceramic bowl, combine the chicken with the cornflour, soy and oyster sauces and sugar. Cover and refrigerate for 1 hour.

2   Heat the wok until very hot, add 1 tablespoon of the oil and swirl it around to coat the side. Stir-fry the chicken in two batches over high heat for 4–5 minutes, or until cooked. Add oil between batches. Remove all the chicken from the wok and set it aside.

3   Reheat the wok, add 1 tablespoon of the oil and stir-fry the onion over medium–high heat for 3–4 minutes, or until it is slightly softened. Add the garlic, ginger, capsicum, celery, spring onion, mushrooms and water chestnuts to the wok. Stir-fry over high heat for 3–4 minutes.

4   Combine the extra cornflour with the rice wine, chicken stock and soy sauce. Add to the wok and bring to the boil. Simmer for 1–2 minutes, or until the sauce thickens slightly. Stir in the cabbage and cook, covered, for 1–2 minutes, or until the cabbage is just wilted. Return the chicken to the wok and toss until heated through. Season with salt and pepper. Arrange the noodles around the edge of a large platter and spoon the chicken mixture into the centre. Serve immediately, garnished with spring onion.

Combine the cornflour, rice wine, stock and soy sauce and pour into the wok.

NUTRITION PER SERVE (6)
Protein 25 g; Fat 8.5 g; Carbohydrate 20 g; Dietary Fibre 4 g; Cholesterol 55 mg; 1110 kJ (265 Cal)

Chicken with oyster sauce and basil

PREPARATION TIME: 20 MINUTES | TOTAL COOKING TIME: 10 MINUTES | SERVES 4

60 ml (2 fl oz/¼ cup) oyster sauce
2 tablespoons fish sauce
1 tablespoon grated palm sugar (jaggery)
1 tablespoon oil
2–3 garlic cloves, crushed
1 tablespoon grated fresh ginger
1–2 red chillies, seeded and finely chopped
4 spring onions (scallions), finely chopped
375 g (13 oz) boneless, skinless chicken
    breasts, cut into thin strips
250 g (9 oz) broccoli, cut into florets
230 g (8 oz) tin water chestnuts, drained
230 g (8 oz) tin sliced bamboo shoots, rinsed
20 basil leaves, shredded

1   Put 60 ml (2 fl oz/¼ cup) water in a small bowl with the oyster sauce, fish sauce and palm sugar. Mix well.

2   Heat the wok until very hot, add the oil and swirl it around to coat the side. Stir-fry the garlic, ginger, chilli and spring onion for 1 minute over medium heat. Increase the heat to medium–high, add the chicken and stir-fry for 2–3 minutes, or until it is just cooked. Remove from the wok.

3   Reheat the wok and add the broccoli, water chestnuts and bamboo shoots. Stir-fry for 2–3 minutes, tossing constantly. Add the sauce and bring to the boil, tossing constantly. Return the chicken to the wok and toss until it is heated through. Stir in the basil and serve at once.

Palm sugar is bought in a block. Grate it or crush with the back of a large knife.

Wearing disposable gloves to prevent skin irritation, remove the seeds from the chilli and chop finely.

NUTRITION PER SERVE
Protein 30 g; Fat 3.5 g; Carbohydrate 35 g; Dietary Fibre 8 g; Cholesterol 45 mg; 1205 kJ (285 Cal)

Butter chicken

PREPARATION TIME: 10 MINUTES | TOTAL COOKING TIME: 35 MINUTES | SERVES 4–6

2 tablespoons peanut oil
1 kg (2 lb 4 oz) boneless, skinless chicken
    thighs, cubed
60 g (2¼ oz) salted butter
2 teaspoons garam masala
2 teaspoons sweet paprika
2 teaspoons ground coriander
1 tablespoon finely chopped fresh ginger
¼ teaspoon chilli powder
1 cinnamon stick
6 cardamom pods, bruised
350 g (12 oz) tomato passata
    (puréed tomatoes)
1 tablespoon sugar
60 g (2¼ oz/¼ cup) plain yoghurt
125 ml (4 fl oz/½ cup) pouring
    (whipping) cream
1 tablespoon lemon juice

1 Heat a wok until very hot, add 1 tablespoon oil and swirl to coat the side of the wok. Stir-fry the chicken in two batches, for 4 minutes each batch, or until browned. Remove from the wok.

2 Reduce the heat and add the butter to the wok. Add the spices and stir-fry for 1 minute, or until fragrant. Add the chicken and and stir to coat in the spices.

3 Add the tomato and sugar and simmer, stirring, for 15 minutes, or until the chicken is tender and the sauce is thick. Add the yoghurt, cream and lemon juice, and warm through for 5 minutes. Remove the cinnamon stick and cardamom pods before serving.

Bruise the cardamom pods by crushing them with the back of a knife to release the flavour.

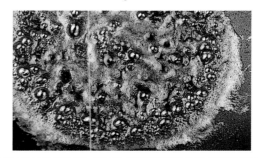
Melt the butter in the wok, then stir-fry the spices for 1 minute, or until fragrant.

NUTRITION PER SERVE (6)
Protein 32 g; Fat 27 g; Carbohydrate 7.5 g; Dietary Fibre 1 g; Cholesterol 122 mg; 1669 kJ (397 Cal)

Sichuan pepper chicken

PREPARATION TIME: 25 MINUTES + 2 HOURS MARINATING | TOTAL COOKING TIME: 20 MINUTES | SERVES 4

3 teaspoons sichuan peppercorns
500 g (1 lb 2 oz) boneless, skinless chicken
    thighs, cut into strips
2 tablespoons soy sauce
1 garlic clove, crushed
1 teaspoon grated fresh ginger
3 teaspoons cornflour (cornstarch)
100 g (3½ oz) dried thin egg noodles
oil, for cooking
1 onion, sliced
1 yellow capsicum (pepper), cut into
    thin strips
1 red capsicum (pepper), cut into thin strips
100 g (3½ oz) sugar snap peas
60 ml (2 fl oz/¼ cup) chicken stock

NUTRITION PER SERVE
Protein 35 g; Fat 15 g; Carbohydrate 25 g; Dietary
Fibre 3 g; Cholesterol 65 mg; 1515 kJ (360 Cal)

1 Heat the wok until very hot and dry-fry the sichuan peppercorns for 30 seconds. Remove from the wok and crush with a mortar and pestle or in a spice mill or small food processor.

2 Combine the chicken strips with the soy sauce, garlic, ginger, cornflour and sichuan pepper in a bowl. Cover and refrigerate for 2 hours.

3 Cook the egg noodles in boiling water for 5 minutes, or until tender. Drain, then drizzle with a little oil and toss it through the noodles to prevent them from sticking together. Set aside.

4 Heat the wok until very hot, add 1 tablespoon of the oil and swirl it around to coat the side. Stir-fry the chicken in batches over medium–high heat for 5 minutes, or until golden brown and cooked. Add more oil when necessary. Remove from the wok and set aside.

5 Reheat the wok, add 1 tablespoon of the oil and stir-fry the onion, capsicum and sugar snap peas over high heat for 2–3 minutes, or until the vegetables are tender. Add the chicken stock and bring to the boil.

6 Return the chicken and egg noodles to the wok and toss over high heat. Serve immediately.

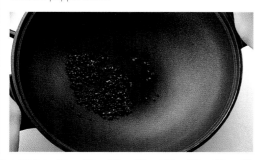

Heat the wok until very hot, then dry-fry the sichuan peppercorns.

Crush the sichuan peppercorns with a mortar and pestle or in a spice mill.

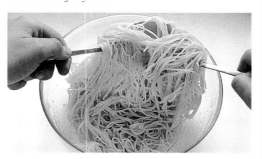

Toss the oil through the noodles to prevent them from sticking together.

Chicken with soy and hokkien noodles

PREPARATION TIME: 10 MINUTES + 10 MINUTES STANDING | TOTAL COOKING TIME: 10 MINUTES | SERVES 4

450 g (1 lb) hokkien (egg) noodles
1 tablespoon oil
500 g (1 lb 2 oz) boneless, skinless chicken
 thighs, trimmed and sliced
2 garlic cloves, chopped
5 cm (2 inch) piece fresh ginger, finely
 shredded
4 spring onions (scallions), sliced on
 the diagonal
2 carrots, thinly sliced on the diagonal
250 g (9 oz) broccoli, cut into small florets
2 tablespoons mirin
4 tablespoons soy sauce
1 teaspoon soft brown sugar
2 tablespoons toasted sesame seeds

1 Cover the noodles with boiling water and leave for 10 minutes, or until tender.

2 Heat a wok over high heat, add the oil and swirl to coat the side. Add the chicken in batches and stir-fry for 5 minutes. Return all the chicken to the wok, add the garlic and ginger and cook for 1 minute, or until fragrant. Add the spring onion, carrot and broccoli and cook for 4–5 minutes, or until tender.

3 Mix together the mirin, soy sauce and sugar and stir into the chicken mixture. Drain the noodles, add to the wok and cook until heated through. Serve sprinkled with the sesame seeds.

Add the garlic and ginger to the chicken and stir-fry for a further minute.

Add the spring onion, carrot and broccoli to the wok and cook until tender.

NUTRITION PER SERVE
Protein 64 g; Fat 25 g; Carbohydrate 114 g; Dietary Fibre 12 g; Cholesterol 100 mg; 3930 kJ (939 Cal)

Chicken with snow peas

PREPARATION TIME: 10 MINUTES | TOTAL COOKING TIME: 10 MINUTES | SERVES 4

1 tablespoon oil
2 teaspoons sesame oil
400 g (14 oz) boneless, skinless chicken
    breasts, thinly sliced
1 leek, white part only, finely shredded
2 garlic cloves, crushed
185 g (6¼ oz) snow peas (mangetouts), cut in
    half on the diagonal
2 tablespoons soy sauce
1 tablespoon mirin
1 teaspoon soft brown sugar
coriander (cilantro) leaves, to garnish

1   Heat a wok over high heat, add the oils
and swirl to coat the side. Add the sliced
chicken breast in batches and stir-fry for
3–4 minutes, or until just cooked.

2   Add the leek and garlic and stir-fry for
1–2 minutes, or until the leek is soft and golden.
Add the snow peas and stir-fry for 1 minute.
Add the soy sauce, mirin and sugar to the wok,
and toss well. Season well. Garnish with the
coriander and serve immediately.

Stir-fry the chicken in the combined oils until it is just cooked.

Add the soy sauce, mirin and sugar to the wok and toss well.

NUTRITION PER SERVE
Protein 50 g; Fat 17 g; Carbohydrate 10 g; Dietary
Fibre 4 g; Cholesterol 100 mg; 1664 kJ (398 Cal)

Tangy orange and ginger chicken

PREPARATION TIME: 15 MINUTES | TOTAL COOKING TIME: 15–20 MINUTES | SERVES 4

2 tablespoons sesame seeds (see HINT)
3 tablespoons olive oil
10 boneless, skinless chicken thighs, cut into
    small pieces
3 teaspoons grated fresh ginger
1 teaspoon grated orange zest
125 ml (4 fl oz/½ cup) chicken stock
2 teaspoons honey
500 g (1 lb 2 oz/1 bunch) bok choy
    (pak choy), trimmed and halved

NUTRITION PER SERVE
Protein 70 g; Fat 20 g; Carbohydrate 3.5 g; Dietary
Fibre 0.5 g; Cholesterol 150 mg; 2005 kJ (480 Cal)

1   Toast the sesame seeds by dry-frying them
in the wok, placing under a hot grill (broiler),
or roasting them in a 200°C (400°F/Gas 6)
oven for 5 minutes on a baking tray.

2   Heat a wok over high heat, add the
oil and swirl to coat the side of the wok.
Add the chicken in batches and stir-fry for
3–4 minutes, or until golden.

3   Return all the chicken to the wok, add
the ginger and orange zest and cook for
20 seconds, or until fragrant. Add the stock
and the honey and stir to combine. Increase
the heat and cook for 3–4 minutes, or until the
sauce has thickened slightly.

4   Add the bok choy to the wok and cook
until it has slightly wilted. Season with salt and
black pepper. Sprinkle with the toasted sesame
seeds and serve immediately.

HINT: *Toasting the sesame seeds before use
brings out their flavour.*

Stir-fry the chicken in batches so that the wok
doesn't overcrowd.

Add the stock and honey and cook until the sauce
has thickened slightly.

Vietnamese chicken salad

PREPARATION TIME: 25 MINUTES | TOTAL COOKING TIME: 10 MINUTES | SERVES 6

1 small Chinese cabbage, finely shredded
2 tablespoons oil
2 onions, halved and thinly sliced
500 g (1 lb 2 oz) boneless, skinless chicken
    thighs, trimmed and thinly sliced
60 g (2¼ oz/¼ cup) sugar
60 ml (2 fl oz/¼ cup) fish sauce
80 ml (2½ fl oz/⅓ cup) lime juice
1 tablespoon white vinegar
2 very large handfuls Vietnamese mint or
    common mint, chopped
2 very large handfuls coriander
    (cilantro), chopped, extra leaves, to garnish
Vietnamese mint leaves, extra, to garnish

1 Place the cabbage in a large bowl, cover with plastic wrap and chill.

2 Heat a wok until very hot, add 1 tablespoon of the oil and swirl to coat the side of the wok. Add half the onion and half the chicken, and stir-fry for 4–5 minutes, or until the chicken is cooked. Remove and repeat with the remaining oil, onion and chicken. Cool.

3 To make the dressing, mix together the sugar, fish sauce, lime juice, vinegar and ½ teaspoon salt with a fork. To serve, toss together the cabbage, chicken and onion, dressing, mint and coriander and garnish with the extra coriander and mint leaves.

Finely shred the Chinese cabbage and then leave to chill until ready to serve.

Stir-fry half the onion and half the chicken strips for 4–5 minutes.

NUTRITION PER SERVE
Protein 17 g; Fat 8 g; Carbohydrate 13 g; Dietary Fibre 1.5 g; Cholesterol 35 mg; 805 kJ (190 Cal)

Nonya lime chicken

PREPARATION TIME: 20 MINUTES | TOTAL COOKING TIME: 25 MINUTES | SERVES 4–6

90 g (3¼ oz/¾ cup) Asian shallots (eschalots)
4 garlic cloves, chopped
2 lemongrass stems, white part only, chopped
2 teaspoons finely chopped fresh galangal
1 teaspoon ground turmeric
2 tablespoons sambal oelek (South-East Asian chilli paste)
1 tablespoon shrimp paste
60 ml (2 fl oz/¼ cup) oil
1 kg (2 lb 4 oz) boneless, skinless chicken thighs, cut into cubes
400 ml (14 fl oz) coconut milk
1 teaspoon finely grated lime zest
125 ml (4 fl oz/½ cup) lime juice
6 makrut (kaffir lime) leaves, finely shredded
2 tablespoons tamarind concentrate
lime wedges and shredded makrut (kaffir lime) leaves, to garnish

1   Place the shallots, garlic, lemongrass, galangal, turmeric, sambal oelek and shrimp paste in a blender and blend until smooth.

2   Heat a wok until very hot, add the oil and swirl to coat the side of the wok. Add the spice paste and stir-fry for 1–2 minutes, or until fragrant. Add the chicken and stir-fry for 5 minutes, or until browned.

3   Add the coconut milk, lime zest and juice, makrut leaves and tamarind concentrate. Reduce the heat and simmer for 15 minutes, or until the chicken is cooked and the sauce has reduced and thickened slightly. Season well with salt. Garnish with lime wedges and shredded makrut leaves to serve.

Fresh galangal is similar to fresh ginger. Peel it and then finely chop or grate.

Blend the shallots, garlic, lemongrass, galangal, turmeric, sambal oelek and shrimp paste.

NUTRITION PER SERVE (6)
Protein 32 g; Fat 25 g; Carbohydrate 4 g; Dietary Fibre 1.5 g; Cholesterol 65 mg; 1590 kJ (380 Cal)

Chicken nasi goreng

PREPARATION TIME: 25 MINUTES | TOTAL COOKING TIME: 15 MINUTES | SERVES 4–6

5–8 long red chillies, seeded and chopped

2 teaspoons shrimp paste

8 garlic cloves, finely chopped

oil, for cooking

2 eggs, lightly beaten

350 g (12 oz) boneless, skinless chicken thighs, cut into thin strips

200 g (7 oz) raw prawns (shrimp), peeled and deveined

1.5 kg (3 lb 5 oz/8 cups) cooked rice

80 ml (2½ fl oz/⅓ cup) kecap manis (see NOTE, page 18)

80 ml (2½ fl oz/⅓ cup) soy sauce

2 small Lebanese (short) cucumbers, chopped

1 large tomato, chopped

lime wedges, to serve

1 Mix the chilli, shrimp paste and garlic in a food processor until the mixture resembles a paste.

2 Heat the wok until very hot, add 1 tablespoon of the oil and swirl it around to coat the side. Add the beaten eggs and, using a wok chan or metal egg flip, push the egg up the edges of the wok to form a large omelette. Cook for 1 minute over medium heat, or until the egg is set, then flip it over and cook the other side for 1 minute. Remove from the wok and cool before slicing into strips.

3 Reheat the wok, add 1 tablespoon of the oil and stir-fry the chicken and half the chilli paste over high heat until the chicken is just cooked. Remove the chicken from the wok.

4 Reheat the wok, add 1 tablespoon of the oil and stir-fry the prawns and the remaining chilli paste until the prawns are cooked. Remove from the wok and set aside.

5 Reheat the wok, add 1 tablespoon of the oil and the cooked rice, and toss constantly over medium heat for 4–5 minutes, or until the rice is heated through. Add the kecap manis and soy sauce, and toss constantly until all of the rice is coated in the sauces. Return the chicken and prawns to the wok, and toss until heated through. Season well with freshly cracked pepper and salt. Transfer to a large deep serving bowl and top with the omelette strips, cucumber and tomato. Serve with the lime wedges.

NUTRITION PER SERVE (6)
Protein 30 g; Fat 10 g; Carbohydrate 70 g; Dietary Fibre 3.5 g; Cholesterol 140 mg; 2105 kJ (505 Cal)

Wear disposable gloves to prevent skin irritation, remove the seeds from the chillies and finely chop.

Slit the peeled prawns down the backs to remove the veins.

Process the chilli, shrimp paste and garlic until they form a paste.

Sesame chicken and leek

PREPARATION TIME: 15 MINUTES | TOTAL COOKING TIME: 16 MINUTES | SERVES 4–6

2 tablespoons sesame seeds

1 tablespoon oil

2 teaspoons sesame oil

800 g (1 lb 12 oz) chicken tenderloins (underbelly fillets), thinly sliced

1 leek, white part only, finely shredded, plus extra to garnish

2 garlic cloves, crushed

2 tablespoons soy sauce

1 tablespoon mirin

1 teaspoon sugar

1 Heat the wok until very hot, add the sesame seeds and dry-fry over high heat until they are golden. Remove the seeds from the wok.

2 Reheat the wok, add the oils and swirl them around to coat the side of the wok. Stir-fry the chicken strips in three batches over high heat, tossing constantly until just cooked. Reheat the wok before each addition. Return all the chicken to the wok.

3 Add the shredded leek and the garlic and cook for 1–2 minutes, or until the leek is soft and golden. Check that the chicken is cooked through: if it is not cooked, reduce the heat and cook, covered, for 2 minutes, or until it is completely cooked.

4 Add the soy sauce, mirin, sugar and toasted sesame seeds to the wok, and toss well to combine. Season with salt and black pepper, and serve immediately, garnished with shredded leek. Delicious with pasta.

The tenderloins are the small strips from under the chicken breasts. Slice them diagonally.

Very finely shred the white part of the leek only.

NUTRITION PER SERVE (6)
Protein 30.8 g; Fat 8.5 g; Carbohydrate 3.8 g; Dietary Fibre 1 g; Cholesterol 107 mg; 914 kJ (218 Cal)

Thai red curry noodles and chicken

PREPARATION TIME: 25 MINUTES | TOTAL COOKING TIME: 10–15 MINUTES | SERVES 4–6

200 g (7 oz) thick rice stick noodles
1½ tablespoons oil
1 tablespoon red curry paste
3 boneless, skinless chicken thighs, thinly
   sliced
1–2 teaspoons chopped red chillies
2 tablespoons fish sauce
2 tablespoons lime juice
100 g (3½ oz) bean sprouts
90 g (3¼ oz/½ cup) roasted chopped peanuts
3 tablespoons crisp-fried onion
3 tablespoons crisp-fried garlic
2 very large handfuls coriander
   (cilantro) leaves

1   Cook the noodles in boiling water for 2 minutes. Drain and then toss with 2 teaspoons of the oil to prevent them from sticking together.

2   Heat the remaining oil in a wok, add the curry paste and stir for 1 minute, or until fragrant. Add the chicken in batches and stir-fry for 2 minutes, or until golden brown. Return all the chicken to the wok.

3   Add the chilli, fish sauce and lime juice, bring to the boil and simmer for 1 minute. Add the bean sprouts and noodles and toss well. Arrange the noodles on a serving plate and sprinkle with peanuts, crisp-fried onion and garlic and coriander leaves. Serve immediately.

HINT: *Rice stick noodles are flat and are available from Asian food stores and some supermarkets.*

NUTRITION PER SERVE (6)
Protein 15 g; Fat 11 g; Carbohydrate 9 g; Dietary Fibre 2 g; Cholesterol 25 mg; 812 kJ (194 Cal)

Toss 2 teaspoons of oil through the noodles to prevent them from sticking together.

Cook each batch of chicken for 2 minutes and return all the chicken to the wok.

Rice sticks with chicken and greens

PREPARATION TIME: 25 MINUTES | TOTAL COOKING TIME: 10 MINUTES | SERVES 4

6 baby bok choy (pak choy)

8 stems Chinese broccoli

150 g (5½ oz) dried rice stick noodles

2 tablespoons oil

375 g (13 oz) boneless, skinless chicken
     breasts or tenderloins (underbelly fillets),
     thinly sliced

2–3 garlic cloves, crushed

5 cm (2 inch) piece fresh ginger, grated

6 spring onions (scallions), cut into
     short pieces, plus extra finely shredded
     spring onion, to garnish

1 tablespoon sherry

90 g (3¼ oz/1 cup) bean sprouts

SAUCE

2 teaspoons cornflour (cornstarch)

2 tablespoons soy sauce

2 tablespoons oyster sauce

2 teaspoons soft brown sugar

1 teaspoon sesame oil

1   Remove any tough outer leaves from the bok choy and Chinese broccoli. Cut the leaves and stems into bite-sized pieces. Wash well, then drain and dry thoroughly.

2   Place the rice stick noodles in a large heatproof bowl and cover with boiling water. Soak for 5–8 minutes, or until softened. Rinse, then drain. Cut into short lengths.

3   Meanwhile, to make the sauce, mix the cornflour and soy sauce to a smooth paste, then stir in the oyster sauce, brown sugar, sesame oil and 125 ml (4 fl oz/½ cup) water.

4   Heat the wok until very hot, add the oil and swirl it around to coat the side. Stir-fry the chicken, garlic, ginger and spring onion in batches over high heat for 3–4 minutes, or until the chicken is cooked. Remove from the wok.

5   Add the chopped bok choy, Chinese broccoli and sherry to the wok, cover and steam for 2 minutes, or until wilted. Remove from the wok. Add the sauce to the wok and stir until glossy and slightly thickened. Return the chicken, vegetables, noodles and bean sprouts to the wok, and stir until heated through. Serve at once, topped with shredded spring onion.

HINT: *Instead of the Chinese broccoli and bok choy, you can use broccoli and English spinach as the greens.*

NUTRITION PER SERVE
Protein 30 g; Fat 15 g; Carbohydrate 50 g; Dietary
Fibre 4 g; Cholesterol 45 mg; 1855 kJ (445 Cal)

Cut the leaves and stems of the bok choy and
Chinese broccoli into pieces.

Using a pair of scissors, cut the soaked noodles
into short lengths.

Honey chicken

PREPARATION TIME: 15 MINUTES | TOTAL COOKING TIME: 25 MINUTES | SERVES 4

oil, for cooking
500 g (1 lb 2 oz) boneless, skinless chicken
   thighs, cubed
1 egg white, lightly beaten
40 g (1½ oz/⅓ cup) cornflour (cornstarch)
2 onions, thinly sliced
1 green capsicum (pepper), cut into batons
2 carrots, cut into batons
100 g (3½ oz) snow peas (mangetouts), sliced
90 g (3¼ oz/¼ cup) honey
2 tablespoons toasted almonds

1 Heat the wok until very hot, add
1½ tablespoons of the oil and swirl it around
to coat the side. Dip half of the chicken into the
egg white, then lightly dust with the cornflour,
shaking off any excess. Stir-fry in batches over
high heat for 4–5 minutes, or until the chicken is
golden brown and just cooked. Remove from the
wok and drain on paper towels. Repeat with the
remaining chicken, then remove all the chicken
from the wok.

2 Reheat the wok, add 1 tablespoon of the
oil and stir-fry the sliced onion over high heat
for 3–4 minutes, or until slightly softened. Add
the capsicum and carrot and cook, tossing
constantly, for 3–4 minutes, or until tender. Stir
in the snow peas and cook for 2 minutes.

3 Increase the heat, add the honey and toss the
vegetables until well coated. Return the chicken
to the wok and toss until it is heated through
and is well coated in the honey. Remove from the
heat and season well with salt and pepper. Serve
immediately, sprinkled with the almonds.

Trim the excess fat from the chicken and cut the
chicken into cubes.

Dip the chicken into the egg white, then lightly dust
with the cornflour.

NUTRITION PER SERVE
Protein 35 g; Fat 20 g; Carbohydrate 35 g; Dietary
Fibre 4 g; Cholesterol 60 mg; 1815 kJ (435 Cal)

Chicken and asparagus

PREPARATION TIME: 15 MINUTES | TOTAL COOKING TIME: 10 MINUTES | SERVES 4

2 tablespoons oil
1 garlic clove, crushed
10 cm (4 inch) piece fresh ginger, peeled and
   thinly sliced
3 boneless, skinless chicken breasts, sliced
4 spring onions (scallions), sliced, plus extra
   finely shredded spring onion, to garnish
200 g (7 oz) fresh asparagus spears, cut into
   short lengths
2 tablespoons soy sauce
30 g (1 oz/⅓ cup) slivered almonds, roasted

1 Heat a wok over high heat, add the oil and swirl to coat the side. Add the garlic, ginger and chicken and stir-fry in batches for 1–2 minutes, or until the chicken changes colour.

2 Add the spring onion and asparagus and stir-fry for a further 2 minutes, or until the spring onion is soft.

3 Stir in the soy sauce and 60 ml (2 fl oz/ ¼ cup) water, cover and simmer for 2 minutes, or until the chicken is tender and the vegetables are slightly crisp. Sprinkle with the almonds and serve immediately, topped with shredded spring onion.

NUTRITION PER SERVE
Protein 30 g; Fat 12 g; Carbohydrate 2 g; Dietary
Fibre 1 g; Cholesterol 60 mg; 1010 kJ (240 Cal)

Stir-fry the garlic, ginger and chicken until the chicken changes colour.

Add the spring onion and asparagus and stir-fry until the spring onion is soft.

Stir in the soy sauce and a little water and cover the wok to steam the vegetables.

Chicken with walnuts and straw mushrooms

PREPARATION TIME: 20 MINUTES | TOTAL COOKING TIME: 15 MINUTES | SERVES 4

375 g (13 oz) boneless, skinless chicken breasts or tenderloins (underbreast fillets), thinly sliced
½ teaspoon five-spice powder
2 teaspoons cornflour (cornstarch)
2 tablespoons soy sauce
2 tablespoons oyster sauce
2 teaspoons soft brown sugar
1 teaspoon sesame oil
oil, for cooking
70 g (2½ oz) walnuts
150 g (5½ oz) snake beans or green beans, chopped
425 g (15 oz) tin straw mushrooms, rinsed
6 spring onions (scallions), sliced, plus extra finely shredded spring onion, to garnish
225 g (8 oz) tin sliced bamboo shoots, rinsed

NUTRITION PER SERVE
Protein 30 g; Fat 25 g; Carbohydrate 10 g; Dietary Fibre 6.5 g; Cholesterol 45 mg; 1675 kJ (400 Cal)

1 Dry the chicken with paper towels and sprinkle with five-spice powder. Mix the cornflour with the soy sauce in a bowl until smooth. Add 125 ml (4 fl oz/½ cup) water and the oyster sauce, brown sugar and sesame oil.

2 Heat the wok until very hot, add 1 tablespoon of the oil and swirl it around to coat the side. Stir-fry the walnuts for 30 seconds, or until lightly browned. Drain on paper towels.

3 Reheat the wok and add 1 tablespoon of the oil. Stir-fry the chicken in batches over high heat for 2–3 minutes, or until just cooked through. Remove all the chicken from the wok and set aside.

4 Add the snake beans, straw mushrooms, spring onion and bamboo shoots to the wok and stir-fry for 2 minutes. Remove from the wok. Add the soy sauce mixture and heat for 1 minute, or until slightly thickened. Return the chicken and vegetables to the wok, and toss to coat with the sauce. Season well. Serve at once, sprinkled with the fried walnuts and garnished with shredded spring onion.

Wash the straw mushrooms in a sieve under cold running water.

Top and tail the snake beans, and then cut them into pieces.

Cook the walnuts in the oil until they are lightly browned. Sprinkle them over the stir-fry.

Noodles with chicken and black beans

PREPARATION TIME: 15 MINUTES | TOTAL COOKING TIME: 15 MINUTES | SERVES 2–3

2 teaspoons salted black beans

oil, for cooking

2 teaspoons sesame oil

500 g (1 lb 2 oz) boneless, skinless chicken
thighs, thinly sliced

3 garlic cloves, very thinly sliced

4 spring onions (scallions), chopped, plus
extra finely shredded spring onion, to
garnish

1 teaspoon sugar

1 red capsicum (pepper), sliced

100 g (3½ oz) green beans, cut into
short pieces

300 g (10½ oz) hokkien (egg) noodles

2 tablespoons oyster sauce

1 tablespoon soy sauce

1   Rinse the black beans in running water. Drain
and roughly chop.

2   Heat the wok until very hot, add
1 tablespoon of oil and the sesame oil and swirl
it around to coat the side. Stir-fry the chicken
in three batches, until well browned, tossing
regularly. Remove from the wok and set aside.

3   Reheat the wok, add 1 tablespoon of the
oil and stir-fry the garlic and spring onion for
1 minute. Add the black beans, sugar, capsicum
and green beans, and cook for 1 minute. Sprinkle
with 2 tablespoons of water, cover and steam
for 2 minutes.

4   Gently separate the noodles and add to
the wok with the chicken, oyster sauce and soy
sauce, and toss well. Cook, covered, for about
2 minutes, or until the noodles are just softened.
Top with shredded spring onion.

Cut the chicken thighs into thin strips, removing
any excess fat.

Rinse the salted black beans under running water,
then roughly chop them.

NUTRITION PER SERVE (3)
Protein 50 g; Fat 20 g; Carbohydrate 50 g; Dietary
Fibre 2 g; Cholesterol 85 mg; 2490 kJ (595 Cal)

Ginger chicken with black fungus

PREPARATION TIME: 25 MINUTES | TOTAL COOKING TIME: 15 MINUTES | SERVES 4

3 tablespoons black fungus (see HINT)
1 tablespoon oil
3 garlic cloves, chopped
5 cm (2 inch) piece fresh ginger, shredded
500 g (1 lb 2 oz) boneless, skinless chicken
    breasts, sliced
4 spring onions (scallions), chopped
1 tablespoon soy sauce
1 tablespoon fish sauce
2 teaspoons soft brown sugar
½ red capsicum (pepper), finely sliced
1 small handful coriander (cilantro) leaves
1 small handful Thai basil leaves, shredded

1   Place the fungus in a bowl of hot water for 15 minutes until it is soft and swollen; drain and chop roughly.

2   Heat the oil in a large wok and stir-fry the garlic and ginger for 1 minute. Add the chicken in batches, stir-frying over high heat until it is cooked. Return all the chicken to the wok. Add the spring onion and soy sauce and cook for 1 minute.

3   Add the fish sauce, brown sugar and fungus to the wok. Toss well, cover and steam for 2 minutes. Serve immediately, scattered with red capsicum, coriander and basil.

HINT: *Black fungus is a dried mushroom that swells to many times its size when soaked in hot water. It is available from Asian food speciality stores and is also known as 'wood ear' or 'cloud ear' mushroom.*

When the fungus is soft and swollen, drain it well and chop it with a sharp knife.

Add the spring onions and soy sauce and stir-fry for 1 minute.

NUTRITION PER SERVE
Protein 29.2 g; Fat 6.5 g; Carbohydrate 5.1 g; Dietary Fibre 1.6 g; Cholesterol 81 mg; 836 kJ (200 Cal)

Country chicken kapitan

PREPARATION TIME: 35 MINUTES I TOTAL COOKING TIME: 35 MINUTES I SERVES 4–6

30 g (1 oz) small dried prawns (shrimp)

4 tablespoons oil

4–8 red chillies, seeded and finely chopped, plus extra finely chopped chilli, to garnish

4 garlic cloves, finely chopped

3 lemongrass stems, white part only, finely chopped

2 teaspoons ground turmeric

10 candlenuts

2 large onions, chopped

250 ml (9 fl oz/1 cup) coconut milk

500 g (1 lb 2 oz) boneless, skinless chicken thighs, cut into bite-sized pieces

125 ml (4 fl oz/½ cup) coconut cream

2 tablespoons lime juice

1 Dry-fry the prawns over low heat for 3 minutes, shaking the wok regularly, until they are dark orange and have a strong aroma. Pound in a mortar and pestle until finely ground, or process in a small food processor.

2 Mix half the oil with the chilli, garlic, lemongrass, turmeric and candlenuts in a food processor, in short bursts, regularly scraping the bowl, until very finely chopped.

3 Add the remaining oil to a large wok and cook the onion and ¼ teaspoon salt over low heat, stirring regularly, for 8 minutes, or until golden. Add the spice mixture and nearly all the ground prawns, setting a little aside to use as garnish. Stir for 5 minutes. If the mixture begins to stick to the bottom of the wok, add 2 tablespoons of the coconut milk. It is important for the flavour to cook this thoroughly.

4 Add the chicken and stir well. Cook for 5 minutes, or until the chicken begins to brown. Stir in the coconut milk and 250 ml (9 fl oz/ 1 cup) water and bring to the boil. Reduce the heat and simmer for 7 minutes, or until the chicken is cooked and the sauce is thick. Add the coconut cream and bring back to the boil, stirring constantly. Add the lime juice and serve immediately, sprinkled with the reserved ground prawns and sliced chilli.

NUTRITION PER SERVE (6)
Protein 22 g; Fat 15 g; Carbohydrate 5.5 g; Dietary Fibre 2.5 g; Cholesterol 50 mg; 1020 kJ (245 Cal)

Pound the dry-fried prawns in a mortar and pestle until finely ground.

Process the chilli mixture in shorts bursts, regularly scraping the side of the bowl.

Stir-fry the onion and spice mixture for 5 minutes, taking care not to let it stick.

Thai chicken and basil

PREPARATION TIME: 15 MINUTES | TOTAL COOKING TIME: 7 MINUTES | SERVES 4

3 tablespoons fish sauce
3 tablespoons lime juice
1 tomato, diced
1 very large handful Thai basil leaves
2 tablespoons peanut or vegetable oil
3 garlic cloves, thinly sliced
4 spring onions (scallions), finely sliced
2 small red chillies, seeded and thinly sliced
4 boneless, skinless chicken breasts,
    thinly sliced
250 g (9 oz) snow peas (mangetouts), trimmed

1   Place the fish sauce, lime juice, tomato, basil and 1 tablespoon water in a small bowl and mix well.

2   Heat a wok over high heat, add the oil and swirl to coat the side. Add the garlic, spring onion and chilli and stir-fry for 1 minute, or until fragrant. Add the chicken and cook for 3 minutes, or until lightly browned.

3   Add the snow peas and the fish sauce mixture and scrape any bits from the bottom of the wok. Reduce the heat and simmer for 2 minutes, or until the tomato is soft and the chicken cooked through. Serve immediately.

NUTRITION PER SERVE
Protein 57 g; Fat 20 g; Carbohydrate 10 g; Dietary Fibre 6.5 g; Cholesterol 110 mg; 1887 kJ (450 Cal)

Mix together the fish sauce, lime juice, tomato, basil and water.

Add the chicken to the wok and stir-fry until it is lightly browned.

Simmer until the tomato is soft and the chicken is cooked through.

Wok-fried chicken and lemongrass

PREPARATION TIME: 15 MINUTES | TOTAL COOKING TIME: 12 MINUTES | SERVES 4

1 tablespoon fish sauce

3 teaspoons grated palm sugar (jaggery)

1 tablespoon peanut oil

2 teaspoons sesame oil

800 g (1 lb 12 oz) boneless, skinless chicken
    breasts, cut into strips

1½ tablespoons grated fresh ginger

2 tablespoons finely chopped lemongrass,
    white part only

2 garlic cloves, finely chopped

2 tablespoons coriander (cilantro) leaves

2 limes, cut into wedges

1   Place the fish sauce and palm sugar in a small
bowl and stir until all the sugar has dissolved.

2   Heat a large wok until very hot, add half the
combined oils and swirl to coat. Add half the
chicken and stir-fry for 4 minutes, then remove.
Repeat with the remaining oil and the second
batch of chicken and then remove from the wok.

3   Add the ginger, lemongrass and garlic to
the wok and stir-fry for 1–2 minutes, then
return all the chicken to the wok and stir-fry for
2 minutes more.

4   Stir in the combined fish sauce and palm
sugar. Scatter with the coriander leaves and serve
immediately with the lime wedges.

Palm sugar is bought in blocks. Grate the sugar,
using an ordinary cheese grater.

Cut the chicken breasts into strips and then stir-fry
in two batches.

NUTRITION PER SERVE
Protein 45 g; Fat 15 g; Carbohydrate 2 g; Dietary
Fibre 0 g; Cholesterol 100 mg; 1330 kJ (318 Cal)

Caramel coriander chicken

PREPARATION TIME: 20 MINUTES + OVERNIGHT REFRIGERATION | TOTAL COOKING TIME: 20 MINUTES | SERVES 4–6

2 teaspoons ground turmeric

6 garlic cloves, crushed

2 tablespoons grated fresh ginger

2 tablespoons soy sauce

60 ml (2 fl oz/¼ cup) Chinese rice wine
  or sherry

2 egg yolks, beaten

1 kg (2 lb 4 oz) boneless, skinless chicken
  thighs, cut into cubes

60 g (2¼ oz/½ cup) plain (all-purpose) flour

125 ml (4 fl oz/½ cup) oil

90 g (3¼ oz/½ cup) soft brown sugar

2 very large handfuls coriander
  (cilantro), chopped, plus extra leaves, to
  garnish

60 ml (2 fl oz/¼ cup) rice vinegar

NUTRITION PER SERVE (6)
Protein 35 g; Fat 25 g; Carbohydrate 30 g; Dietary
Fibre 2 g; Cholesterol 130 mg; 2070 kJ (495 Cal)

1 Place the turmeric, 2 crushed garlic cloves, the ginger, soy sauce, rice wine, egg yolks, 1 teaspoon salt and 1 teaspoon white pepper in a large bowl and mix together well. Add the chicken and toss to coat. Cover with plastic wrap and refrigerate overnight.

2 Pour away any excess liquid from the chicken, add the flour and toss to mix well.

3 Heat a wok until very hot, add 1 tablespoon of the oil and swirl to coat. Add a third of the chicken and stir-fry for 4 minutes, or until golden brown. Remove from the wok. Cook the other two batches of chicken, adding more oil as necessary. Remove all the chicken from the wok and keep warm.

4 Reduce the heat to medium, add the remaining oil, brown sugar and remaining garlic. Mix together and then leave for 1–2 minutes, or until the sugar caramelises and liquefies.

5 Return the chicken to the wok, and add the coriander and vinegar. Stir gently for 4 minutes, or until the chicken is cooked through and well coated with the sauce. Garnish with extra coriander leaves.

Cut the chicken thighs into bite-sized cubes for even stir-frying.

Mix together the turmeric, garlic, ginger, soy sauce, rice wine, egg yolks, salt and pepper.

Leave the sauce to cook until the sugar caramelises and liquefies.

Peppered chicken

PREPARATION TIME: 10 MINUTES | TOTAL COOKING TIME: 10 MINUTES | SERVES 4

1 tablespoon oil
2 boneless, skinless chicken breasts,
   cut into strips
2½ teaspoons seasoned peppercorns
   (see HINT)
1 onion, cut into wedges
1 red capsicum (pepper), cut into strips
2 tablespoons oyster sauce
1 teaspoon soy sauce
1 teaspoon sugar

1   Heat a wok over high heat, add the oil and swirl to coat the base and side of the wok. Add the chicken strips and stir-fry for 2–3 minutes, or until they are browned.

2   Add the peppercorns and stir-fry until they are fragrant. Add the onion and capsicum and stir-fry for 2 minutes, or until the vegetables have softened slightly.

3   Reduce the heat and stir in the oyster sauce, soy sauce and sugar. Toss well to thoroughly combine before serving.

HINT: *Seasoned peppercorns are available in the herb and spice section of large supermarkets.*

NUTRITION PER SERVE
Protein 18 g; Fat 6.5 g; Carbohydrate 6 g; Dietary Fibre 1 g; Cholesterol 40 mg; 665 kJ (160 Cal)

Add the strips of chicken breast to the wok and stir-fry until browned.

Add the onion and capsicum and stir-fry until they have softened slightly.

Add the oyster sauce, soy sauce and sugar to the stir-fry and toss through.

Chicken san choy bau

PREPARATION TIME: 10 MINUTES | TOTAL COOKING TIME: 5 MINUTES | SERVES 4 AS A STARTER

1 tablespoon oil

700 g (1 lb 9 oz) minced (ground) chicken

2 garlic cloves, finely chopped

100 g (3½ oz) tin water chestnuts, drained, chopped

1½ tablespoons oyster sauce

3 teaspoons soy sauce

1 teaspoon sugar

5 spring onions (scallions), finely sliced, plus extra finely shredded spring onion, to garnish

4 lettuce leaves

1 Heat a wok over high heat, add the oil and swirl to coat the base and side of the wok. Add the minced chicken and garlic and stir-fry for 3–4 minutes, or until browned and cooked through, breaking up any lumps with the back of a spoon. Pour off any excess liquid.

2 Reduce the heat and add the water chestnuts, oyster sauce, soy sauce, sugar and spring onion.

3 Trim the lettuce leaves around the edges to neaten them and to form each one into a cup shape. Divide the chicken mixture among the lettuce cups and serve hot, with extra oyster sauce if you like. Garnish with the spring onion.

NUTRITION PER SERVE
Protein 40 g; Fat 9 g; Carbohydrate 6 g; Dietary
Fibre 2 g; Cholesterol 88 mg; 1142 kJ (273 Cal)

Stir-fry the minced chicken, breaking up any lumps with the back of a spoon.

Add the water chestnuts, oyster sauce, soy sauce, sugar and spring onion.

Trim the edges of the lettuce leaves and form them into cup shapes to hold the chicken mixture.

Soy chicken and crisp noodles

PREPARATION TIME: 30 MINUTES | TOTAL COOKING TIME: 35 MINUTES | SERVES 4–6

750 g (1 lb 10 oz) boneless, skinless
    chicken thighs
3 teaspoons cornflour (cornstarch)
80 ml (2½ fl oz/⅓ cup) soy sauce
oil, for deep-frying
100 g (3½ oz) dried rice vermicelli
1 garlic clove, crushed
2 teaspoons grated fresh ginger
1 carrot, sliced
2 celery stalks, sliced
1 red capsicum (pepper), sliced
1 green capsicum (pepper), sliced
100 g (3½ oz) snow peas (mangetouts),
    trimmed
6 spring onions (scallions), sliced, plus extra
    finely shredded spring onion, to garnish
60 ml (2 fl oz/¼ cup) chicken stock

NUTRITION PER SERVE (6)
Protein 30 g; Fat 9 g; Carbohydrate 20 g; Dietary
Fibre 2 g; Cholesterol 85 mg; 1150 kJ (275 Cal)

1 Cut the chicken into 2 cm (¾ inch) cubes. Mix the cornflour with half the soy sauce, add the chicken, then cover and refrigerate until ready to use.

2 Heat the oil in a large pan. Break the vermicelli into small pieces. Drop a noodle into the oil: if it fizzes and puffs, the oil is hot enough. Add the noodles in small amounts and cook until puffed and white. Drain on paper towels and set aside.

3 Heat 1 tablespoon of the oil in a wok, add the chicken and stir-fry in batches over high heat for about 4 minutes, or until cooked. Remove the chicken from the wok and set aside.

4 Heat 1 tablespoon of the oil in the wok and cook the garlic and ginger for 30 seconds. Add the vegetables and cook, tossing well, for 2–3 minutes.

5 Add the chicken, stock and remaining soy sauce and stir until boiled and thickened. Transfer to serving plates and arrange the noodles around the outside of the plates. Garnish with the spring onion.

Mix the cornflour with half the soy sauce and then add the chicken and leave to marinate.

To test if the oil is hot, add one noodle. If the noodle fizzes and puffs, the oil is hot enough.

Cook the noodles in the hot oil until they are puffed and white.

Lemon chicken

PREPARATION TIME: 15 MINUTES + 30 MINUTES MARINATING | TOTAL COOKING TIME: 10 MINUTES | SERVES 4

1 egg white, lightly beaten
2 teaspoons cornflour (cornstarch)
¼ teaspoon grated fresh ginger
500 g (1 lb 2 oz) boneless, skinless chicken
    breasts, sliced
3 tablespoons oil

LEMON SAUCE
2 teaspoons cornflour (cornstarch)
1½ tablespoons caster (superfine) sugar
2 tablespoons lemon juice
185 ml (6 fl oz/¾ cup) chicken stock
2 teaspoons soy sauce
1 teaspoon dry sherry
lemon zest, to garnish

1 Combine the egg white, cornflour, ½ teaspoon salt and ginger in a bowl. Add the chicken and mix well to coat in the marinade. Leave in the fridge to marinate for 30 minutes.

2 Heat the oil in a wok, swirling gently to coat the side. Drain the chicken, discarding the marinade, and stir-fry until just cooked but not browned. Remove from the wok.

3 To make the lemon sauce, mix the cornflour with 2 tablespoons water to make a smooth paste. Add to the wok with the remaining sauce ingredients. Stir and boil for 1 minute. Return the chicken to the wok and stir to coat with the sauce. Serve immediately, garnished with lemon zest.

Cut the chicken breasts into strips on the diagonal —they will hold together better.

Drain the chicken from the marinade and stir-fry until just cooked but not browned.

NUTRITION PER SERVE
Protein 30 g; Fat 15 g; Carbohydrate 10 g; Dietary Fibre 0 g; Cholesterol 65 mg; 1315 kJ (315 Cal)

Sweet chilli chicken

PREPARATION TIME: 10 MINUTES | TOTAL COOKING TIME: 10 MINUTES | SERVES 4–6

375 g (13 oz) hokkien (egg) noodles
4 boneless, skinless chicken thighs, cut into
    small pieces (see HINT)
1–2 tablespoons sweet chilli sauce
2 teaspoons fish sauce
1 tablespoon oil
100 g (3½ oz) baby sweet corn,
    halved lengthways
150 g (5½ oz) sugar snap peas
1 tablespoon lime juice
chilli, to garnish

1   Place the noodles in a large bowl, cover with boiling water and gently pull apart with a fork. Leave for 5 minutes, then drain.

2   Combine the chicken, sweet chilli sauce and fish sauce in a bowl.

3   Heat a wok over high heat, add the oil and swirl to coat. Add the chicken pieces and stir-fry for 3–5 minutes, or until cooked through. Add the corn and sugar snap peas and stir-fry for 2 minutes. Add the noodles and lime juice and serve, topped with sliced chilli.

HINT: *If thighs are unavailable, use 3 breasts.*

NUTRITION PER SERVE (6)
Protein 30 g; Fat 6.5 g; Carbohydrate 50 g; Dietary
Fibre 4 g; Cholesterol 53 mg; 1593 kJ (380 Cal)

Soak the noodles in boiling water and separate them with a fork.

Mix together the chicken pieces, sweet chilli sauce and fish sauce.

Mix together the chicken and vegetables, noodles and lime juice.

Chicken with beans and asparagus

PREPARATION TIME: 25 MINUTES + AT LEAST 15 MINUTES MARINATING | TOTAL COOKING TIME: 15 MINUTES | SERVES 4

1 lemongrass stem, white part only, chopped

5 cm (2 inch) piece fresh ginger, peeled and chopped

2–3 small red chillies, seeded and chopped

1 teaspoon grated makrut (kaffir lime) or lime zest

2–3 garlic cloves, chopped

2 tablespoons oil

375 g (13 oz) boneless, skinless chicken breasts, thinly sliced

250 g (9 oz) green beans, cut into short pieces

1 celery stalk, cut into short slices

185 g (6½ oz) snow peas (mangetouts), halved

200 g (7 oz) asparagus, cut into short pieces

270 ml (9½ fl oz) tin coconut cream

2 tablespoons sweet chilli sauce

20 small basil leaves

1 Place the lemongrass, ginger, chilli, makrut or lime zest, garlic, ½ teaspoon ground black pepper and oil in a food processor or blender and process until the mixture forms a rough paste. Combine the paste and chicken strips in a glass or ceramic bowl, cover and refrigerate for at least 15 minutes.

2 Briefly blanch the beans, celery, snow peas and asparagus in a pan of boiling water. Drain and plunge into iced water. Drain again.

3 Heat the wok until very hot and stir-fry the chicken mixture in batches over high heat for 3–4 minutes, or until the chicken is cooked through. Stir constantly so the paste doesn't burn. Add the vegetables, coconut cream, sweet chilli sauce to taste, and basil leaves. Stir-fry until heated through. Serve with rice or noodles.

NUTRITION PER SERVE
Protein 50 g; Fat 30 g; Carbohydrate 8 g; Dietary Fibre 6 g; Cholesterol 95 mg; 1990 kJ (475 Cal)

Grating citrus zest is easier and less wasteful if you fit a piece of baking paper over the grater.

Process the lemongrass, ginger, chilli, zest, garlic, pepper and oil to a paste.

Curried chicken noodles

PREPARATION TIME: 20 MINUTES | TOTAL COOKING TIME: 10 MINUTES | SERVES 4

100 g (3½ oz) dried rice vermicelli

oil, for cooking

500 g (1 lb 2 oz) boneless, skinless chicken
    breasts, thinly sliced

2 garlic cloves, crushed

1 teaspoon grated fresh ginger

2 teaspoons Asian-style curry powder

1 red onion, sliced

1 red capsicum (pepper), cut into short
    thin strips

2 carrots, cut into matchsticks

2 zucchini (courgettes), cut into matchsticks

1 tablespoon soy sauce

1 Cover the vermicelli with boiling water and soak for 5 minutes. Drain well and place on a tea towel (dish towel) to dry.

2 Heat the wok until very hot, add 1 tablespoon of the oil and swirl it around to coat the side. Stir-fry the chicken in batches over high heat until browned and tender. Remove all the chicken and drain on paper towels.

3 Reheat the wok, add 1 tablespoon of oil and stir-fry the garlic, ginger, curry powder and onion for 1–2 minutes, or until fragrant. Add the capsicum, carrot and zucchini and stir-fry until well coated with the spices. Add 1 tablespoon water and stir-fry for 1 minute.

4 Add the drained noodles and chicken to the wok. Add the soy sauce and toss well. Season and serve.

Trim any excess fat from the chicken and cut the chicken into thin strips.

Cut the carrot into strips that are the size and shape of matchsticks.

NUTRITION PER SERVE
Protein 30 g; Fat 15 g; Carbohydrate 25 g; Dietary Fibre 4 g; Cholesterol 60 mg; 1495 kJ (355 Cal)

Chicken with snow pea sprouts

PREPARATION TIME: 15 MINUTES | TOTAL COOKING TIME: 15 MINUTES | SERVES 4

2 tablespoons oil
1 onion, finely sliced
3 makrut (kaffir lime) leaves, shredded
   (see HINT)
3 boneless, skinless chicken breasts, cubed
1 red capsicum (pepper), sliced
60 ml (2 fl oz/¼ cup) lime juice
100 ml (3½ fl oz) soy sauce
100 g (3½ oz) snow pea (mangetout) sprouts
2 tablespoons chopped coriander (cilantro)
   leaves

1 Heat a wok over medium heat, add the oil and swirl to coat the side of the wok. Add the onion and makrut leaves and stir-fry for 3–5 minutes, or until the onion begins to soften. Add the chicken and cook for a further 4 minutes. Add the capsicum and continue to cook for 2–3 minutes.

2 Stir in the lime juice and soy sauce and cook for 1–2 minutes, or until the sauce reduces slightly. Add the sprouts and coriander and cook until the sprouts have wilted slightly. Serve immediately.

HINT: *Makrut leaves are quite tough leaves with a wonderful aroma and flavour. Because of their toughness, however, it is necessary to shred them as finely as possible. Fold the leaves in half down their spines and then shred finely with a very sharp knife.*

VARIATION: *Use fresh asparagus instead of capsicum, and mint or basil instead of coriander.*

NUTRITION PER SERVE
Protein 45 g; Fat 15 g; Carbohydrate 5.5 g; Dietary Fibre 2 g; Cholesterol 90 mg; 1375 kJ (330 Cal)

Add the chicken and cook for 4 minutes, then add the capsicum.

Add the snow pea sprouts and coriander and cook until they have wilted a little.

Orange chilli chicken in lettuce cups

PREPARATION TIME: 35–40 MINUTES | TOTAL COOKING TIME: 10–15 MINUTES | SERVES 4

500 g (1 lb 2 oz) minced (ground) chicken
1 tablespoon soy sauce
1 tablespoon rice wine vinegar
1 tablespoon sesame oil
peanut oil, for deep-frying
60 g (2¼ oz) dried rice vermicelli noodles, broken into sections
1 red capsicum (pepper), finely chopped
120 g (4¼ oz) tin water chestnuts, drained and roughly chopped
2 spring onions (scallions), finely sliced, plus extra finely shredded spring onion, to garnish
1 teaspoon grated fresh ginger
1 iceberg (or romaine) lettuce

SAUCE
2 tablespoons soy sauce
1 tablespoon teriyaki sauce
1 tablespoon mild–hot chilli sauce
2 tablespoons hoisin sauce
1 teaspoon sesame oil
2 teaspoons finely grated orange zest
1 teaspoon cornflour (cornstarch)

1 Mix together the minced chicken, soy sauce, vinegar and sesame oil, cover and refrigerate until ready to cook.

2 Half-fill a deep-fryer or large pan with oil and heat to moderately hot. Add the rice noodles in small batches (they increase in size rapidly, causing the oil to rise) and fry for 1–2 seconds, or until puffed. Remove and drain on paper towels.

3 To make the sauce, combine all the ingredients and stir until the cornflour has dissolved. Set aside.

4 Heat a little peanut oil in a wok. Add the chicken mixture and fry for 3–4 minutes, breaking up any lumps with a fork or wooden spoon. Add the capsicum, water chestnuts, spring onion and ginger to the wok and toss for 1–2 minutes. Add the sauce to the wok and stir for about 1 minute, or until slightly thickened. Remove from the heat and mix in the noodles, reserving a few for garnish. Form the lettuce leaves into 6–8 cups and divide the chicken mixture among them. Sprinkle the reserved noodles on top and garnish with the extra spring onion.

NUTRITION PER SERVE
Protein 30 g; Fat 10 g; Carbohydrate 12 g; Dietary Fibre 3 g; Cholesterol 65 mg; 1095 kJ (260 Cal)

Finely chop the capsicum and slice 2 spring onions, including the green tops.

Use a slotted spoon to remove the cooked noodles from the pan.

Use a wooden spoon or fork to break up any lumps of minced chicken as it cooks.

Chilli-crusted chicken noodles

PREPARATION TIME: 25 MINUTES | TOTAL COOKING TIME: 20 MINUTES | SERVES 4–6

1½ teaspoons chilli powder

3 tablespoons cornflour (cornstarch)

2 tablespoons oil

350 g (12 oz) boneless, skinless chicken thighs, sliced

4 spring onions (scallions), sliced, plus extra finely shredded spring onion, to garnish

1 carrot, sliced

1 celery stalk, sliced

2 tablespoons mirin or sherry

500 g (1 lb 2 oz) hokkien (egg) noodles, gently pulled apart

2 tablespoons oyster sauce

250 g (9 oz) baby bok choy (pak choy), washed, trimmed, leaves separated

1 Combine the chilli powder, cornflour and 1½ teaspoons salt and mix well. Heat the oil in a wok over high heat. Coat the chicken strips in the cornflour mix and stir-fry in batches for 3 minutes each batch, or until golden. Remove all the chicken from the wok and drain on paper towels.

2 Reheat the wok over medium heat. Add the spring onion, carrot and celery and stir-fry for 1 minute. Add the mirin and the noodles, tossing well until the vegetables have softened.

3 Add the oyster sauce and 2 tablespoons water, cover and steam for 2–4 minutes, or until the noodles are tender.

4 Add the chicken and bok choy and toss well. Cover and steam for 30 seconds only. Serve immediately topped with shredded spring onion.

Gently pull apart the hokkien noodles before you cook them.

Coat the chicken in the mixture of cornflour, chilli powder and salt.

NUTRITION PER SERVE (6)
Protein 15 g; Fat 9 g; Carbohydrate 30 g; Dietary Fibre 3 g; Cholesterol 40 mg; 1165 kJ (275 Cal)

Quick Thai chicken

PREPARATION TIME: 15 MINUTES | TOTAL COOKING TIME: 15 MINUTES | SERVES 4

1 tablespoon red curry paste

2 tablespoons oil

2 tablespoons fish sauce

2 tablespoons lime juice

1 very large handful coriander (cilantro) leaves, chopped, plus extra leaves, to garnish

1 tablespoon grated fresh ginger

1 teaspoon caster (superfine) sugar

1 teaspoon sesame oil

750 g (1 lb 10 oz) boneless, skinless chicken thighs, sliced

1 tablespoon oil, extra

10 spring onions (scallions), cut into short lengths

100 g (3½ oz) snow peas (mangetouts), trimmed

1 Whisk together the curry paste, oil, fish sauce, lime juice, coriander, ginger, sugar and sesame oil in a large non-metallic bowl. Add the chicken strips and toss to coat thoroughly.

2 Heat the extra oil in a wok. Add the chicken in batches and stir-fry for 3–5 minutes, or until browned all over, then remove from the wok and set aside. Add the spring onion and snow peas and stir-fry for 2 minutes. Return the chicken and any juices to the wok and stir-fry for 2–3 minutes, or until the chicken is heated through. Season with salt and pepper, sprinkle with coriander leaves and serve.

Brown the chicken in batches so that the wok doesn't overcrowd and cool down.

Stir-fry the spring onion and snow peas for 2 minutes before adding the cooked chicken.

NUTRITION PER SERVE
Protein 45 g; Fat 10 g; Carbohydrate 6 g; Dietary Fibre 2.5 g; Cholesterol 95 mg; 1275 kJ (305 Cal)

Seafood

Salt-and-pepper squid

PREPARATION TIME: 40 MINUTES + 20 MINUTES MARINATING | TOTAL COOKING TIME: 10 MINUTES | SERVES 4

500 g (1 lb 2 oz) squid tubes
80 ml (2½ fl oz/⅓ cup) oil
4 garlic cloves, finely chopped
½ teaspoon sugar
2 teaspoons sea salt
1 teaspoon ground black pepper
150 g (5½ oz) baby English spinach leaves
100 g (3½ oz) cherry tomatoes, quartered
2 tablespoons lime juice
lime quarters, to garnish

1   Cut the squid tubes in half lengthways and open them out. Rinse and pat dry with paper towels. Lay on a chopping board with the inside facing upwards. Honeycomb the squid by scoring along the length of each piece very finely, then diagonally across the width to create a fine diamond pattern. Cut the squid into pieces 5 x 3 cm (2 x 1¼ inches). Combine the squid, oil, garlic, sugar and half the salt and pepper, cover and refrigerate for 20 minutes.

2   Arrange the spinach leaves and tomatoes on a large serving platter.

3   Heat the wok until it is very hot and stir-fry the squid in several batches over high heat, tossing constantly, for 1–2 minutes, or until the squid just turns white and curls. Keep the wok very hot and don't cook the squid for too long or it will toughen.

4   Return all the squid pieces to the wok with the lime juice and the remaining salt and pepper. Stir briefly until heated through. Arrange on top of the spinach and garnish with the lime wedges. Serve immediately.

NUTRITION PER SERVE
Protein 20 g; Fat 15 g; Carbohydrate 3 g; Dietary Fibre 2 g; Cholesterol 250 mg; 1020 kJ (250 Cal)

Cut the squid tubes in half lengthways, and open them out.

Score very finely along the length, then diagonally to create a diamond pattern.

Fold the honeycombed squid tubes over and cut them into pieces.

Spicy chilli prawns

PREPARATION TIME: 20 MINUTES + OVERNIGHT MARINATING | TOTAL COOKING TIME: 5 MINUTES | SERVES 4

20–24 raw prawns (shrimp), unpeeled
crusty bread and lemon wedges, to serve

MARINADE
1 small red onion, finely chopped
125 ml (4 fl oz/½ cup) olive oil
1 tablespoon grated lime or lemon zest
2–3 garlic cloves, crushed
125 ml (4 fl oz/½ cup) lime or lemon juice
2–3 small red chillies, seeded and
    finely chopped
1 tablespoon grated fresh ginger
1 lemongrass stem, white part only,
    finely chopped
1 teaspoon ground turmeric

1   Place the prawns in a large glass or
ceramic bowl. Mix the marinade ingredients,
add to the prawns and toss well. Cover and
refrigerate overnight. Turn the prawns once or
twice while marinating.

2   Drain the prawns, reserving the marinade.
Heat the wok until very hot and stir-fry the
prawns in three batches over high heat until they
are pink and very crisp. Remove from the wok.

3   Pour the reserved marinade into the wok.
Bring to the boil, then return the prawns to the
wok and toss well. Season and serve immediately.

HINT: *The whole prawn, including the crisp shell,
can be eaten. If you prefer, you can discard the
prawn heads before marinating.*

Toss the whole prawns in the marinade before
refrigerating overnight.

Drain the prawns in a sieve, so that you can keep
the marinade.

NUTRITION PER SERVE
Protein 25 g; Fat 30 g; Carbohydrate 30 g; Dietary
Fibre 3 g; Cholesterol 150 mg; 2150 kJ (515 Cal)

Malay fish curry

PREPARATION TIME: 25 MINUTES | TOTAL COOKING TIME: 25 MINUTES | SERVES 4

3–6 red chillies, chopped, to taste, plus extra
    finely sliced, to garnish
1 onion, chopped
4 garlic cloves, chopped
3 lemongrass stems, white part only, sliced
5 cm (2 inch) piece fresh ginger, peeled and
    sliced
2 teaspoons shrimp paste
60 ml (2 fl oz/¼ cup) oil
1 tablespoon fish curry powder (see NOTE)
250 ml (9 fl oz/1 cup) coconut milk
1 tablespoon tamarind concentrate
1 tablespoon kecap manis (see NOTE,
    page 18)
350 g (12 oz) firm white fish fillets, cut into
    bite-sized pieces
2 ripe tomatoes, chopped
1 tablespoon lemon juice

1 Combine the chillies, onion, garlic, lemongrass, ginger and shrimp paste in a small food processor and process until roughly chopped. Add 2 tablespoons of the oil and process to a smooth paste.

2 Heat the remaining oil in a wok and add the paste. Cook for 3–4 minutes over low heat, stirring constantly, until very fragrant. Add the curry powder and stir for another 2 minutes. Add the coconut milk, tamarind, kecap manis and 250 ml (9 fl oz/1 cup) water to the wok. Bring to the boil, stirring occasionally, then reduce the heat and simmer for 10 minutes.

3 Add the fish, tomato and lemon juice and season well. Simmer for 5 minutes, or until the fish is just cooked. Serve immediately, garnished with sliced chilli.

NOTE: *Fish curry powder is a blend of spices suited to seafood flavours. It is available from Asian food stores.*

NUTRITION PER SERVE
Protein 22 g; Fat 30 g; Carbohydrate 6.5 g; Dietary
Fibre 4 g; Cholesterol 65 mg; 1600 kJ (382 Cal)

Process the ingredients to make a smooth paste, then stir-fry over low heat for 3–4 minutes.

Add the coconut milk to the paste and simmer the sauce for 10 minutes, stirring occasionally.

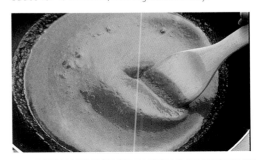

Curried lobster with capsicum

PREPARATION TIME: 25 MINUTES | TOTAL COOKING TIME: 15 MINUTES | SERVES 4

2 raw lobster tails
1 tablespoon oil
1–2 tablespoons red curry paste, to taste
2 lemongrass stems, white part only,
    finely chopped
1 red capsicum (pepper), roughly chopped
250 ml (9 fl oz/1 cup) coconut milk
6 dried Chinese black dates (see NOTE)
1 tablespoon fish sauce
2 teaspoons soft brown sugar
1 teaspoon grated lime zest
coriander (cilantro) leaves, to garnish

NUTRITION PER SERVE
Protein 28 g; Fat 13 g; Carbohydrate 9 g; Dietary
Fibre 1.2 g; Cholesterol 136 mg; 1075 kJ (255 Cal)

1   To remove the meat from the lobster, cut down the centre of each lobster tail on the underside. Pull away the shell, remove the flesh and cut into bite-sized pieces.

2   Heat the oil in a wok and swirl to coat the base and side. Add the curry paste and lemongrass and stir-fry for 1 minute over medium heat. Add the lobster pieces a few at a time and stir-fry each batch for 2 minutes, just until golden brown. Remove from the wok.

3   Add the capsicum to the wok and stir-fry for 30 seconds. Add the coconut milk and dates, bring to the boil and cook for 5 minutes, or until the dates are plump.

4   Add the fish sauce, brown sugar and lime zest to the curry. Return the lobster to the wok to heat through. Serve immediately, sprinkled with coriander leaves.

NOTE: *You can buy dried Chinese black dates from Asian food stores.*

Use kitchen scissors to cut down the centre of the lobster tails on the underside.

Stir-fry the lobster pieces in batches for 2 minutes, or until golden brown.

Cook the mixture for about 5 minutes, until the dried Chinese dates have plumped up.

Prawn omelette

PREPARATION TIME: 15 MINUTES I TOTAL COOKING TIME: 15 MINUTES I SERVES 2–4

2 tablespoons oil
3 garlic cloves, chopped
2 lemongrass stems, white part only,
    finely chopped
2 coriander (cilantro) roots, finely chopped,
    plus extra leaves, to garnish
1–2 teaspoons chopped red chillies, chopped,
    plus extra finely sliced, to garnish
500 g (1 lb 2 oz) raw prawns
    (shrimp), peeled
3 spring onions (scallions), chopped, plus
    extra finely shredded, to garnish
½ teaspoon black pepper
1½ tablespoons fish sauce
2 teaspoons soft brown sugar
4 eggs
chilli sauce, for serving

1   Heat half the oil in a wok. Add the garlic, lemongrass, coriander root and chilli and stir-fry for 20 seconds. Add the prawns and stir-fry until they change colour. Add the spring onion, pepper, 1 tablespoon of the fish sauce and brown sugar; toss well and remove.

2   Beat the eggs, remaining fish sauce and 2 tablespoons water until foamy. Add the remaining oil to the wok and swirl around to coat the side. Heat the wok and, when it is very hot, pour in the egg mixture and swirl around the wok. Allow the mixture to set underneath, frequently lifting the edge once set, and tilting the wok a little to let the unset mixture run underneath. Repeat until the omelette is nearly set.

3   Place three-quarters of the prawn mixture in the centre of the omelette and fold in the sides to make a square (or simply fold in half). Slide onto a serving plate and place the remaining mixture on top. Garnish and serve with chilli sauce.

Add the chopped spring onions, pepper, fish sauce and brown sugar to the prawns.

Tilt the wok and lift the edge of the omelette to let the unset mixture run underneath.

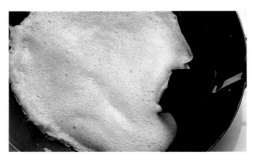

NUTRITION PER SERVE (4)
Protein 30 g; Fat 10 g; Carbohydrate 3 g; Dietary Fibre 1 g; Cholesterol 320 mg; 925 kJ (220 Cal)

Fish cutlets in spicy red sauce

PREPARATION TIME: 10 MINUTES | TOTAL COOKING TIME: 35 MINUTES | SERVES 4

1 tablespoon oil
2 onions, finely chopped
4 ripe tomatoes, peeled and chopped
1 tablespoon sambal oelek (South-East Asian
    chilli paste)
1 tablespoon soft brown sugar
4 blue eyed cod cutlets or other firm
    fish cutlets
2 tablespoons fish sauce
2 tablespoons rice vinegar or white vinegar
2 tablespoons chopped coriander (cilantro)

1   Heat the oil in a wok or large frying pan and add the onion. Cook over medium heat for 2 minutes, or until soft but not browned. Add the tomatoes, sambal oelek, brown sugar and 3 tablespoons of water. Bring to the boil, then reduce the heat, cover the wok and simmer for 20 minutes, or until the sauce is thick.

2   Add the fish cutlets to the wok and spoon sauce over them. Cover and cook for 3–5 minutes. Turn the fish to cook the other side.

3   Transfer the fish to serving plates. Add the fish sauce, vinegar and chopped coriander to the sauce in the wok and stir well before spooning the sauce over the fish.

Place the fish cutlets in the wok, in batches if necessary, and spoon some sauce over.

Transfer the fish to serving plates and add the fish sauce, vinegar and coriander to the wok.

NUTRITION PER SERVE
Protein 20 g; Fat 7 g; Carbohydrate 9 g; Dietary Fibre 2 g; Cholesterol 55 mg; 734 kJ (175 Cal)

Squid in black bean and chilli sauce

PREPARATION TIME: 20 MINUTES | TOTAL COOKING TIME: 10 MINUTES | SERVES 4

4 squid tubes

2 tablespoons oil

1 onion, cut into 8 wedges

1 red capsicum (pepper), sliced

115 g (4 oz) baby corn, halved

3 spring onions (scallions), cut into
   short lengths, plus extra finely shredded
   spring onion, to garnish

BLACK BEAN SAUCE

3 teaspoons cornflour (cornstarch)

2 tablespoons canned salted black beans,
   washed and drained (see NOTE)

2 small red chillies, chopped

2 garlic cloves, crushed

2 teaspoons grated fresh ginger

2 tablespoons oyster sauce

2 teaspoons soy sauce

1 teaspoon sugar

1   Open out each squid tube. Score the flesh of the underside into a diamond pattern. Then cut the squid into 5 cm (2 inch) squares.

2   To make the black bean sauce, mix the cornflour with 125 ml (4 fl oz/½ cup) water until smooth. Mash the black beans with a fork, add the chilli, garlic, ginger, oyster and soy sauces, sugar and the cornflour mix and stir well.

3   Heat the oil in a wok and stir-fry the onion for 1 minute over high heat. Add the capsicum and corn and stir-fry for another 2 minutes.

4   Add the squid to the wok and stir-fry for 1–2 minutes, or until the flesh curls. Add the sauce and bring to the boil, stirring constantly until the sauce thickens. Stir in the spring onion and garnish with the extra spring onion.

NOTE: *Tinned black beans can be bought from Asian food stores. Rinse them well before use.*

NUTRITION PER SERVE
Protein 30 g; Fat 10 g; Carbohydrate 10 g; Dietary Fibre 4 g; Cholesterol 180 mg; 1080 kJ (255 Cal)

Score a shallow diamond pattern over the underside of the squid flesh so that it curls when cooked.

Toss the squid in the wok with the capsicum and corn until the squid begins to curl.

Add the sauce to the wok and bring to the boil, stirring until the sauce thickens.

Fish with ginger

PREPARATION TIME: 20 MINUTES | TOTAL COOKING TIME: 15 MINUTES | SERVES 4

1 tablespoon peanut oil
1 small onion, finely sliced
3 teaspoons ground coriander
600 g (1 lb 5 oz) boneless white fish fillets,
    such as perch, sliced
1 tablespoon finely shredded fresh ginger
1 teaspoon finely chopped and seeded
    green chilli
2 tablespoons lime juice
2 tablespoons coriander (cilantro) leaves

1   Heat a wok until very hot, add the oil and swirl to coat. Add the onion and stir-fry for 4 minutes, or until soft and golden. Add the ground coriander and cook for 1–2 minutes, or until the mixture is fragrant.

2   Add the fish, ginger and chilli, and stir-fry for 5–7 minutes, or until the fish is cooked through. Stir in the lime juice and season. Garnish with the coriander leaves and serve.

NUTRITION PER SERVE
Protein 30 g; Fat 9 g; Carbohydrate 1 g; Dietary Fibre 0.4 g; Cholesterol 105 mg; 895 kJ (214 Cal)

Peel the fresh ginger and then cut the flesh into fine shreds.

Stir-fry the onion for 4 minutes, or until it is soft and golden.

Add the fish, ginger and chilli to the wok and stir-fry until the fish is cooked through.

Prawn salad with makrut

PREPARATION TIME: 20 MINUTES | TOTAL COOKING TIME: 8 MINUTES | SERVES 4

750 g (1 lb 10 oz) large raw prawns (shrimp)
1 tablespoon oil
4 spring onions (scallions), cut into
    short lengths
1 small red chilli, seeded and finely chopped
2 garlic cloves, sliced
2 makrut (kaffir lime) leaves, finely shredded
3 teaspoons grated fresh ginger
3 teaspoons soft brown sugar
2 teaspoons soy sauce
2 tablespoons mirin
2 tablespoons lime juice
mixed lettuce leaves, to serve

1 Peel and devein the prawns, and cut in half lengthways. Heat a wok until very hot, add half the oil and swirl to coat. Add the prawns and stir-fry for 3 minutes, or until nearly cooked.

2 Add the spring onion, chilli, garlic, makrut leaves and ginger. Stir-fry for 1–2 minutes, or until fragrant.

3 Combine the sugar, soy sauce, mirin and lime juice in a bowl, add to the wok and bring to the boil. Serve on the lettuce leaves.

NUTRITION PER SERVE
Protein 1 g; Fat 5 g; Carbohydrate 3.5 g; Dietary
Fibre 1 g; Cholesterol 2 mg; 263 kJ (63 Cal)

Always shred makrut leaves as finely as possible, as they can be tough.

Stir-fry the prawns until they curl up and are almost cooked.

Mix together the sugar, soy sauce, mirin and lime juice and add to the wok.

Sichuan prawns with hokkien noodles

PREPARATION TIME: 20 MINUTES | TOTAL COOKING TIME: 15 MINUTES | SERVES 4

500 g (1 lb 2 oz) hokkien (egg) noodles
2 tablespoons oil
2 garlic cloves, sliced
1 onion, cut into thin wedges
1 tablespoon sichuan peppercorns, crushed
1 lemongrass stem, white part only,
    finely chopped
300 g (10½ oz) green beans, cut into
    short lengths
750 g (1 lb 10 oz) large raw prawns (shrimp),
    peeled, deveined, halved lengthways
2 tablespoons fish sauce
80 ml (2½ fl oz/⅓ cup) oyster sauce
125 ml (4 fl oz/½ cup) chicken stock

1 Cover the noodles with boiling water and stir with a fork to separate them. Leave for a couple of minutes to soften, then drain.

2 Heat a wok until very hot, add 1 tablespoon of the oil and swirl to coat the base and side of the wok. Add the garlic, onion, peppercorns and lemongrass and stir-fry for 2 minutes. Add the beans and stir-fry for 2–3 minutes, or until the beans are tender. Remove the bean and onion mixture from the wok.

3 Reheat the wok, add the remaining oil and swirl to coat the base and side of the wok. Add the prawns and stir-fry for 3–4 minutes, or until just cooked through. Add the bean and onion mixture and the noodles and stir-fry for 3 minutes, or until the noodles are heated through. Add the sauces and stock and bring to the boil. Toss well and serve.

HINT: *Hokkien noodles are also known as fukkien or Singapore noodles. They are thick, yellow and rubbery in texture. Hokkien noodles are made from wheat flour and are cooked and lightly oiled before being packaged for sale.*

NUTRITION PER SERVE
Protein 57 g; Fat 13 g; Carbohydrate 92 g; Dietary Fibre 6 g; Cholesterol 300 mg; 3013 kJ (720 Cal)

Peel and devein the prawns, then cut them in half lengthways.

Cover the noodles with boiling water and stir them with a fork to separate them.

Add the beans and stir-fry for 2–3 minutes, or until they are tender.

Scallops and fish in ginger and lime

PREPARATION TIME: 15 MINUTES I TOTAL COOKING TIME: 15 MINUTES I SERVES 4

500 g (1 lb 2 oz) firm white fish fillets
350 g (12 oz) scallops
2 tablespoons oil
5 cm (2 inch) piece fresh ginger, grated
3 spring onions (scallions), chopped
1 tablespoon lime juice
2 tablespoons chilli jam
2 teaspoons finely grated lime zest
3 tablespoons coriander (cilantro) leaves

1 Cut the fish into bite-sized pieces and remove any black veins from the scallops. Heat half the oil in a wok and stir-fry the ginger and most of the spring onion for 30 seconds. Remove from the wok.

2 Reheat the wok and, when it is very hot, add the remaining oil. Add the fish and scallops in three batches and stir-fry each batch for 2–3 minutes. Remove from the wok and set aside.

3 Add the lime juice, chilli jam, lime zest and 2 tablespoons water to the wok and bring to the boil, stirring. Return the fish, scallops and onion mixture to the wok, tossing gently with the sauce. Serve immediately sprinkled with coriander and the remaining spring onions.

NUTRITION PER SERVE
Protein 37 g; Fat 14 g; Carbohydrate 3 g; Dietary Fibre 0 g; Cholesterol 116 mg; 1185 kJ (283 Cal)

Pull away the large black veins from the scallops.

Stir-fry the fish and scallops in three batches, then remove from the wok.

Return the seafood to the wok and toss gently through the sauce.

Chilli squid with sugar snap peas

PREPARATION TIME: 30 MINUTES | TOTAL COOKING TIME: 10 MINUTES | SERVES 4

500 g (1 lb 2 oz) squid tubes
3 teaspoons grated fresh ginger
2 small red chillies, seeded and finely chopped
1 green chilli, seeded and finely sliced
1 tablespoon green peppercorns in
    brine, drained
oil, for cooking
1 large red capsicum (pepper), cut into strips
1 large green capsicum (pepper), cut
    into strips
1 tablespoon honey
1 tablespoon sweet chilli sauce
200 g (7 oz) sugar snap peas
2 teaspoons grated lime zest

1 Cut the squid tubes in half lengthways and open them out. Rinse and pat dry with paper towels. Place on a chopping board with the inside facing upwards. Cut into thin strips about 5 cm (2 inches) long and 5 mm (¼ inch) wide. Mix with the ginger, chilli, peppercorns and some salt.

2 Heat the wok until very hot, add 1 tablespoon of the oil and swirl it around to coat the side. Stir-fry the squid in three batches for about 2 minutes, or until it turns white. Keep the wok hot and add a little more oil if necessary. Do not overcook the squid or it will toughen. Remove the squid from the wok and set aside.

3 Add the capsicum and toss for 1 minute. Drizzle with the honey and chilli sauce and toss well. Cover and steam for 2 minutes. Add the sugar snap peas, toss well, cover and steam for 1 minute. Add the squid and any juices to the wok with the lime zest and toss well. Serve immediately.

NUTRITION PER SERVE
Protein 25 g; Fat 10 g; Carbohydrate 15 g; Dietary Fibre 4 g; Cholesterol 250 mg; 1075 kJ (255 Cal)

Cut the squid tubes in half lengthways and open them out.

Lay the squid on a chopping board with the inside facing upwards and cut into thin strips.

Fish fillets in coconut milk

PREPARATION TIME: 10 MINUTES | TOTAL COOKING TIME: 15 MINUTES | SERVES 4

2 long green chillies
2 small red chillies
2 lemongrass stems, white part only
2 coriander (cilantro) roots
4 makrut (kaffir lime) leaves (see NOTE, page 33)
2.5 cm (1 inch) piece fresh ginger, thinly sliced
2 garlic cloves, crushed
3 spring onions (scallions), finely sliced
1 teaspoon soft brown sugar
250 ml (9 fl oz/1 cup) coconut milk
400 g (14 oz) firm white fish fillets, cut into bite-sized pieces
125 ml (4 fl oz/½ cup) coconut cream
1 tablespoon fish sauce
2–3 tablespoons lime juice

1 Heat a wok until hot, then add the whole chillies and roast until just beginning to brown. Remove from the wok, cool and slice.

2 Bruise the lemongrass and coriander roots by crushing them with the flat side of a knife.

3 Add the lemongrass, coriander roots, makrut leaves, ginger, garlic, spring onion, sugar and coconut milk to the wok. Stir and bring to the boil. Reduce the heat and simmer for 2 minutes. Add the fish pieces and simmer gently for 2–3 minutes, or until the fish is tender. Stir in the coconut cream.

4 Stir through the chopped green and red chillies, fish sauce, salt and lime juice to taste and serve immediately.

NUTRITION PER SERVE
Protein 23 g; Fat 22 g; Carbohydrate 6.5 g; Dietary Fibre 2.5 g; Cholesterol 70 mg; 1323 kJ (316 Cal)

Roast the whole chillies in a hot wok until they begin to brown.

Bruise the lemongrass and coriander roots by crushing them with the flat side of a knife.

Add the fish pieces to the wok and simmer gently for 2–3 minutes.

Fried clams in roasted chilli paste

PREPARATION TIME: 15 MINUTES | TOTAL COOKING TIME: 15 MINUTES | SERVES 4

ROASTED CHILLI PASTE

2 tablespoons vegetable oil
2 spring onions (scallions), sliced
2 garlic cloves, sliced
85 g (3 oz/¼ cup) small dried prawns (shrimp)
6 small red chillies, seeded
2 teaspoons palm sugar (jaggery)
2 teaspoons fish sauce
2 teaspoons tamarind concentrate

3 garlic cloves, finely sliced
3 small red chillies, seeded and sliced
1 tablespoon light soy sauce
250 ml (9 fl oz/1 cup) chicken stock
1 kg (2 lb 4 oz) clams (vongole), scrubbed
1 medium handful Thai basil leaves

1 To make the roasted chilli paste, heat the oil in a wok and fry the spring onion, garlic, prawns and chilli until golden brown. Remove with a slotted spoon and reserve the oil.

2 Place the spring onion, garlic, prawns, chilli and sugar in a mortar and pestle or small food processor and grind until well blended. Add the fish sauce, tamarind and a pinch of salt. Blend or grind to a finely textured paste.

3 Heat the reserved oil in the wok. Add the garlic, chilli, roasted chilli paste and soy sauce. Mix well, then add the chicken stock and bring just to the boil. Add the clams and cook over medium–high heat for 2–3 minutes. Discard any unopened clams. Sprinkle with the basil leaves and serve immediately.

Use a slotted spoon to remove the onion, garlic, prawns and chillies from the wok.

Blend or grind the mixture to obtain a finely textured paste.

NUTRITION PER SERVE
Protein 30 g; Fat 15 g; Carbohydrate 90 g; Dietary Fibre 5 g; Cholesterol 280 mg; 2490 kJ (700 Cal)

Black bean scallops in ginger chilli oil

PREPARATION TIME: 10–15 MINUTES | TOTAL COOKING TIME: 8 MINUTES | SERVES 4

GINGER CHILLI OIL
80 ml (2½ fl oz/⅓ cup) peanut oil
3 dried red chillies, crushed
2.5 cm (1 inch) piece fresh ginger, grated,
    extra, to garnish
1 garlic clove, thinly sliced
1 tablespoon sesame oil
1 tablespoon soy sauce
2 tablespoons peanut oil
2.5 cm (1 inch) piece fresh ginger, extra, cut
    into paper-thin strips
1 kg (2 lb 4 oz) scallops, cleaned
2 tablespoons salted black beans, rinsed well
60 ml (2 fl oz/¼ cup) dry sherry
1 red capsicum (pepper), cut into strips
90 g (3¼ oz) baby English spinach leaves

1 To make the ginger chilli oil, heat the peanut oil, chilli, ginger and garlic in a pan over medium heat, stirring constantly, for 2 minutes, or until the mixture begins to sizzle. Add the sesame oil and soy sauce and cook for 2 minutes. Cool slightly, then strain and set aside.

2 Heat the peanut oil in a wok over very high heat. Add the extra ginger, stir for a few seconds then cook the scallops in small batches, tossing frequently until they are just cooked through. Remove from the wok.

3 Stir-fry the black beans, sherry and capsicum for 1–2 minutes, then return the scallops to the pan to warm through. Remove from the heat and arrange the scallops on top of the spinach leaves. Drizzle with the ginger chilli oil, garnish with the extra grated ginger and serve immediately.

Allow the ginger chilli oil to cool slightly, then strain into a bowl and set aside.

Cook the scallops in batches over high heat, tossing them frequently.

NUTRITION PER SERVE
Protein 35 g; Fat 35 g; Carbohydrate 5 g; Dietary Fibre 5 g; Cholesterol 80 mg; 2035 kJ (485 Cal)

Black bean and chilli mussels

PREPARATION TIME: 10 MINUTES | TOTAL COOKING TIME: 8 MINUTES | SERVES 4

3 teaspoons salted black beans, rinsed
1 tablespoon shredded fresh ginger
2 garlic cloves, chopped
1 tablespoon sugar
2 tablespoons oyster sauce
1 teaspoon soy sauce
2 teaspoons oil
1 small red chilli, seeded and thinly sliced
1.25 kg (2 lb 12 oz) black mussels, scrubbed and, debearded (see HINT)
2 teaspoons cornflour (cornstarch)
4 spring onions (scallions), sliced on the diagonal
coriander (cilantro) leaves, to serve

NUTRITION PER SERVE
Protein 38 g; Fat 7.5 g; Carbohydrate 19 g; Dietary Fibre 1.5 g; Cholesterol 243 mg; 1240 kJ (295 Cal)

1 Place the black beans, ginger, garlic, sugar, oyster sauce and soy sauce in a small bowl and mash with a fork.

2 Heat a wok over high heat, add the oil and swirl to coat the side. Add the chilli and stir-fry for 30 seconds, then add the black bean mixture and stir-fry for 1 minute, or until fragrant. Add the mussels and stir-fry for 3–5 minutes, or until they open. Discard any unopened mussels. Reduce the heat to low.

3 Place the cornflour and 125 ml (4 fl oz/ ½ cup) water in a bowl and stir until smooth. Add to the wok and bring to the boil, stirring until the sauce boils and thickens. Stir through the spring onion and coriander leaves.

HINT: *When buying live mussels make sure they are fresh. Live mussels will have tightly closed shells—some may be slightly opened. Give the shells a tap and if they close this will indicate that they are still alive. Discard any with broken or cracked shells. Always buy extra to allow for the ones that are cracked or do not open during cooking.*

Mash together the black beans, ginger, garlic, sugar and oyster and soy sauces.

Stir-fry the mussels for 3–5 minutes, or until they open. When cooked, discard any unopened mussels.

Add the cornflour mixture to the wok and bring to the boil until the sauce thickens.

Garlic and ginger prawns

PREPARATION TIME: 25 MINUTES | TOTAL COOKING TIME: 10 MINUTES | SERVES 4

2 tablespoons oil
1 kg (2 lb 4 oz) raw king prawns (shrimp), peeled, deveined and butterflied, tails left intact
3–4 garlic cloves, finely chopped
5 cm (2 inch) piece fresh ginger, cut into matchsticks
2–3 small red chillies, seeded and finely chopped
6 coriander (cilantro) roots, finely chopped
½ red capsicum (pepper), thinly sliced
2 tablespoons lemon juice
125 ml (4 fl oz/½ cup) white wine
2 teaspoons crushed palm sugar (jaggery)
2 teaspoons fish sauce
chopped spring onion (scallion), to serve

1 Heat the wok until very hot, add the oil and swirl to coat. Stir-fry the prawns, garlic, ginger, chilli and coriander root in two batches for 1–2 minutes over high heat, or until the prawns turn pink. Remove all the prawns from the wok and set aside.

2 Add the capsicum to the wok. Cook over high heat for 2–3 minutes. Add the lemon juice, wine and palm sugar. Cook until the liquid has reduced by two-thirds.

3 Add the prawns and sprinkle with fish sauce. Toss to heat through. Garnish with chopped spring onion to serve.

Butterfly the peeled prawns by cutting a slit down the back and opening them out.

Using a large, sharp knife, finely chop the coriander roots.

NUTRITION PER SERVE
Protein 1 g; Fat 10 g; Carbohydrate 4.5 g; Dietary Fibre 1.5 g; Cholesterol 0 mg; 550 kJ (130 Cal)

Fried Korean noodles with prawns

PREPARATION TIME: 30 MINUTES I TOTAL COOKING TIME: 25 MINUTES I SERVES 4

3 tablespoons sesame seeds

2 tablespoons oil

2 teaspoons sesame oil

4 spring onions (scallions), chopped, plus
    extra finely shredded spring onion, to
    garnish

2 garlic cloves, finely chopped

150 g (5½ oz) raw prawns (shrimp), peeled
    and deveined

2 teaspoons finely chopped red chillies

150 g (5½ oz) firm tofu, diced

100 g (3½ oz) button mushrooms, thinly sliced

1 red capsicum (pepper), cut into thin strips

2 tablespoons shoshoyu

2 teaspoons sugar

300 g (10½ oz) hokkien (egg) noodles

1 Dry-fry the sesame seeds over low heat for 3–4 minutes until golden. Cool and then grind in a mortar and pestle.

2 Combine the oils. Heat half the oil in the wok over medium–high heat. Stir-fry the spring onion, garlic and prawns for 1 minute. Add the chilli and cook for another minute. Remove from the wok.

3 Add the tofu to the wok and stir-fry until lightly golden, then remove. Add the remaining oil to the wok, add the mushrooms and capsicum and stir-fry for 3 minutes, or until just crisp.

4 Add the shoshoyu, sugar, noodles and 2 tablespoons water to the wok. Toss gently to separate and coat the noodles in liquid. Cover and steam for 5 minutes. Add the prawn mixture and tofu and toss for 3 minutes over medium heat. Sprinkle with the crushed sesame seeds, garnish with the spring onion and serve.

NUTRITION PER SERVE
Protein 20 g; Fat 25 g; Carbohydrate 55 g; Dietary Fibre 5 g; Cholesterol 70 mg; 2020 kJ (480 Cal)

Stir-fry the onion, garlic and prawns for a minute and then add the chilli.

Stir-fry the tofu, tossing occasionally, until lightly golden. Remove and set aside.

Baby octopus with ginger and lime

PREPARATION TIME: 30 MINUTES + OVERNIGHT MARINATING | TOTAL COOKING TIME: 10 MINUTES | SERVES 4

500 g (1 lb 2 oz) baby octopus
1 very large handful coriander
    (cilantro), chopped
2 garlic cloves, finely chopped
2 red chillies, seeded and chopped
2 teaspoons grated fresh ginger
2 lemongrass stems, white part only, chopped
1 tablespoon oil
2 tablespoons lime juice
oil, for cooking
550 g (1 lb 4 oz/1 bunch) bok choy
    (pak choy), leaves separated
400 g (14 oz) choy sum, leaves separated
2 garlic cloves, crushed, extra
1 teaspoon grated fresh ginger, extra

NUTRITION PER SERVE
Protein 25 g; Fat 6 g; Carbohydrate 8 g; Dietary
Fibre 2 g; Cholesterol 0 mg; 735 kJ (175 Cal)

1   To prepare the baby octopus, remove the head, cut off the eyes, and remove the gut by slitting the head open. Grasp the body firmly and push the beak out with your index finger. Clean the octopus thoroughly under cold running water and pat dry with paper towels. Cut the head into two or three pieces.

2   Place the octopus, coriander, garlic, chilli, ginger, lemongrass, oil and lime juice in a glass bowl. Cover and refrigerate overnight, or for 2 hours.

3   Heat the wok until very hot, add 1 tablespoon of the oil and swirl it around to coat the side. Stir-fry the vegetables with 1 tablespoon water. Cover and steam until just wilted. Spread on a serving plate.

4   Reheat the wok, add 1 tablespoon of the oil and stir-fry the extra garlic and ginger for 30 seconds, or until fragrant. Add the octopus and stir-fry over high heat for 7–8 minutes, or until cooked through. Serve on top of the wilted greens.

Remove the eyes from the octopus by cutting them off the base of the head.

Remove and discard the beak by pushing it out of the octopus.

Seafood with mirin

PREPARATION TIME: 20 MINUTES | TOTAL COOKING TIME: 15 MINUTES | SERVES 4–6

200 g (7 oz) squid tubes

olive oil, for cooking

350 g (12 oz) raw prawns (shrimp), peeled and
    deveined, tails intact

250 g (9 oz) firm white fish fillets, sliced

250 g (9 oz) scallops, cleaned

2 onions, thinly sliced

3 garlic cloves, finely chopped

2 tablespoons finely grated fresh ginger

1 green capsicum (pepper), thinly sliced

5 spring onions (scallions), diagonally sliced,
    plus extra finely shredded spring onion, to
    garnish

2 tablespoons mirin

1   Rinse and dry the squid tubes and slice
into rings. Heat the wok until very hot, add
2 teaspoons of oil and swirl it around to coat
the side. Stir-fry the prawns and squid rings in
batches over high heat until they change colour.
Remove from the wok.

2   Reheat the wok, add 2 teaspoons of the oil
and stir-fry the fish strips and scallops until just
cooked. Do not overcook the seafood or it will
break up. Remove from the wok.

3   Reheat the wok, add 1 tablespoon of the
oil and stir-fry the sliced onion over medium–
high heat for 3–4 minutes, or until it has just
softened. Add the garlic, ginger, capsicum and
spring onion. Increase the heat to high and toss
constantly for 3–4 minutes.

4   Add the mirin and ½ teaspoon salt to the
wok with some cracked pepper, and toss well.
Return all of the seafood to the wok and toss
until well combined and heated through. Serve,
garnished with the spring onion.

Peel the prawns, leaving the tails intact, and pull
out the dark veins from the backs.

Wash and dry the squid tubes and then slice them
into rings.

NUTRITION PER SERVE (6)
Protein 30 g; Fat 8.5 g; Carbohydrate 2 g; Dietary
Fibre 1 g; Cholesterol 195 mg; 880 kJ (210 Cal)

Swordfish with bok choy

PREPARATION TIME: 20 MINUTES I TOTAL COOKING TIME: 10 MINUTES I SERVES 4

cracked black pepper, for coating
500 g (1 lb 2 oz) swordfish steak, cubed
oil, for cooking
3 garlic cloves, thinly sliced
1 onion, sliced
1 kg (2 lb 4 oz) baby bok choy (pak choy),
    leaves separated
100 g (3½ oz) shiitake mushrooms, sliced
2 tablespoons hoisin sauce
2 tablespoons rice wine
1 tablespoon oyster sauce
1 tablespoon soy sauce
1 tablespoon toasted sesame seeds
1 teaspoon sesame oil

1   Dip the swordfish in 2 tablespoons cracked
black pepper until coated, then shake off
any excess.

2   Heat the wok until very hot, add
2 tablespoons of the oil and swirl it around
to coat the side. Stir-fry the swordfish in batches
over high heat until tender. Do not overcook or
the fish will break up. Remove from the wok and
keep warm.

3   Reheat the wok, add 1 tablespoon of the oil
and stir-fry the garlic until crisp and golden. Add
the onion and stir-fry until golden. Add the bok
choy and mushrooms and cook until the leaves
wilt. Combine the hoisin sauce, rice wine, oyster
sauce and soy sauce, pour into the wok and heat.

4   Return the swordfish to the wok and toss.
Serve sprinkled with sesame seeds and drizzled
with the oil.

NUTRITION PER SERVE
Protein 35 g; Fat 15 g; Carbohydrate 15 g; Dietary
Fibre 3 g; Cholesterol 90 mg; 1490 kJ (355 Cal)

Use a sharp knife to cut the swordfish steak into
bite-sized cubes.

Wipe the mushrooms with a damp paper towel,
then cut into slices.

Scallops with black bean sauce

PREPARATION TIME: 15 MINUTES | TOTAL COOKING TIME: 10 MINUTES | SERVES 4–6

600 g (1 lb 5 oz) large scallops, without roe
2 tablespoons cornflour (cornstarch)
80 ml (2½ fl oz/⅓ cup) peanut oil, plus
    1 teaspoon, extra
3 spring onions (scallions), cut into
    short lengths, plus extra finely shredded
    spring onion, to garnish
1 teaspoon finely chopped fresh ginger
2 garlic cloves, crushed
60 g (2¼ oz/¼ cup) salted black beans,
    rinsed, roughly chopped
2 tablespoons Chinese rice wine
1 tablespoon rice wine vinegar
1 tablespoon soy sauce
1 teaspoon soft brown sugar
½ teaspoon sesame oil

NUTRITION PER SERVE (6)
Protein 15 g; Fat 15 g; Carbohydrate 7 g; Dietary
Fibre 2 g; Cholesterol 33 mg; 917 kJ (220 Cal)

1   Remove and discard any veins, membrane or hard muscle from the scallops. Toss in the cornflour to coat. Shake off any excess.

2   Heat a wok until very hot, add 1 teaspoon peanut oil and swirl to coat. Add the spring onion and stir-fry for 30 seconds, then remove from the wok.

3   Add 1 tablespoon peanut oil to the hot wok and swirl to coat. Add one-third of the scallops and stir-fry for 1–2 minutes, or until golden and well sealed—no liquid should be released. Remove and set aside. Repeat twice more to seal the rest of the scallops.

4   Add the remaining tablespoon of peanut oil to the hot wok and swirl to coat. Add the ginger, garlic, black beans, rice wine, rice wine vinegar, soy sauce and brown sugar, and stir-fry for 1 minute, or until the sauce boils and thickens slightly.

5   Return the scallops to the wok and stir-fry for 1 minute, or until heated through and the sauce has thickened again. Stir in the spring onion and sesame oil, garnish with the shredded spring onion and serve immediately.

Rinse the black beans under running water, then roughly chop them.

Stir-fry the scallops for a couple of minutes until they are golden and well sealed.

Stir-fry the sauce for 1 minute, or until it comes to the boil and thickens slightly.

Prawn fried rice

PREPARATION TIME: 20 MINUTES I TOTAL COOKING TIME: 15 MINUTES I SERVES 6

oil, for cooking
4 egg whites, lightly beaten
2 garlic cloves, crushed
350 g (12 oz) raw prawns (shrimp), peeled,
    deveined and halved lengthways
100 g (3½ oz) cooked chicken, shredded
80 g (2¾ oz/½ cup) frozen peas
175 g (6 oz) sliced ham, cut into small strips
1 red capsicum (pepper), diced
4 spring onions (scallions), sliced, plus extra
    finely shredded spring onion, to garnish
750 g (1 lb 10 oz/4 cups) cooked white and
    wild rice blend (see HINT)
1½ tablespoons soy sauce
3 teaspoons fish sauce
1½ teaspoons soft brown sugar

1   Heat 2 teaspoons of the oil in a wok and
pour in the egg white. Cook over low heat,
stirring until the egg is just cooked and slightly
scrambled, then remove and set aside.

2   Reheat the wok, add a little more oil and stir-
fry the garlic, prawns, chicken, peas, ham and
capsicum for 3–4 minutes, or until the prawns
are cooked through.

3   Add the spring onion, rice, soy and fish
sauces and sugar and toss for 30 seconds, or
until heated through. Add the egg, toss lightly
and serve, garnished with spring onion.

HINT: *You will need to cook 260 g (9¼ oz/
1⅓ cups) rice to get 4 cupfuls. For fried rice it is
best to steam or boil your rice a day in advance
and leave it in the fridge overnight. This allows
the grains to separate.*

Stir the egg white over low heat until just cooked
and slightly scrambled.

Stir-fry the garlic, prawns, chicken, peas, ham
and capsicum.

NUTRITION PER SERVE
Protein 35 g; Fat 3 g; Carbohydrate 105 g; Dietary
Fibre 4 g; Cholesterol 120 mg; 2500 kJ (600 Cal)

Bean vermicelli and crabmeat

PREPARATION TIME: 20 MINUTES + 20 MINUTES SOAKING | TOTAL COOKING TIME: 15 MINUTES | SERVES 4

200 g (7 oz) dried mung bean vermicelli
    (cellophane noodles)
2 tablespoons oil
10 Asian shallots (eschalots), very finely sliced
3 garlic cloves, finely chopped
2 lemongrass stems, white part only, very
    finely sliced
1 red capsicum (pepper), cut into matchsticks
170 g (6 oz) tin crabmeat, well drained
2 tablespoons fish sauce
2 tablespoons lime juice
2 teaspoons sugar
3 spring onions (scallions), finely sliced

1   Soak the noodles in boiling water for 20 minutes, or until softened. Drain and cut into shorter lengths.

2   Heat the oil in a wok over high heat. Add the shallots, garlic and lemongrass and stir-fry for 2–3 minutes. Add the capsicum and cook for 30 seconds, tossing well. Add the noodles and toss. Cover and steam for 1 minute, or until the noodles are heated through.

3   Add the crabmeat, fish sauce, lime juice and sugar and toss well. Season with salt and pepper, sprinkle with spring onion and serve.

HINT: *Fresh crabmeat is excellent for this recipe. Some fishmongers sell fresh crabmeat in vacuum packs.*

Finely slice the white section of the fresh lemongrass, using a sharp knife.

Snip the noodles several times with kitchen scissors, to make them easier to eat.

NUTRITION PER SERVE
Protein 5.1 g; Fat 9.6 g; Carbohydrate 48.7 g; Dietary Fibre 1.5 g; Cholesterol 21 mg; 1287 kJ (307 Cal)

Warm prawn and scallop salad

PREPARATION TIME: 30 MINUTES | TOTAL COOKING TIME: 15 MINUTES | SERVES 4

2 teaspoons five-spice powder

1–2 small red chillies, chopped

2–3 garlic cloves, crushed

2 teaspoons sesame oil

oil, for cooking

24 raw prawns (shrimp), peeled and deveined, tails intact

20 scallops, cleaned

200 g (7 oz) asparagus, cut into short lengths

150 g (5½ oz) snow peas (mangetouts)

125 g (4½ oz) rocket (arugula) leaves

2 tablespoons light soy sauce

2 tablespoons lemon juice

1 tablespoon mirin

1 tablespoon honey

6 spring onions (scallions), chopped

2 large handfuls coriander (cilantro) leaves, chopped

1 tablespoon sesame seeds, toasted

NUTRITION PER SERVE
Protein 35 g; Fat 20 g; Carbohydrate 10 g; Dietary Fibre 5 g; Cholesterol 170 mg; 1515 kJ (360 Cal)

1 Mix the five-spice powder, chilli, garlic, sesame oil and 2 tablespoons cooking oil in a large glass bowl. Add the prawns and scallops and toss to coat. Cover and refrigerate for at least 10 minutes.

2 Blanch the asparagus and snow peas briefly in a pan of boiling water. Drain and plunge into a bowl of iced water, then drain again. Tear the rocket leaves if they are too big. Arrange the asparagus, snow peas and rocket on four serving plates.

3 Put the soy sauce, lemon juice, mirin, honey and 1 tablespoon oil in a small bowl. Stir to combine.

4 Heat the wok until very hot and stir-fry the prawns, scallops and spring onion over high heat in three or four batches for 3–4 minutes, or until cooked through. Remove from the wok and set aside.

5 Add the sauce and coriander to the wok and bring to the boil. Cook over high heat for 1–2 minutes. Return the seafood to the wok and toss well. Sprinkle with sesame seeds to serve.

Peel the prawns, leaving the tails intact, and pull out the dark veins.

Slice or pull off any vein, membrane or hard white muscle from the scallops.

Seafood with chilli plum sauce

PREPARATION TIME: 30 MINUTES | TOTAL COOKING TIME: 15 MINUTES | SERVES 4

150 g (5½ oz) squid tubes
1 kg (2 lb 4 oz) English spinach
oil, for cooking
500 g (1 lb 2 oz) raw prawns (shrimp), peeled
 and deveined
400 g (14 oz) scallops, cleaned
2 garlic cloves, crushed
1–2 red chillies, seeded and finely chopped
125 ml (4 fl oz/½ cup) plum sauce
1 teaspoon soft brown sugar
2 tablespoons lime juice
3 spring onions (scallions), sliced

1 Rinse the squid tubes, pat dry with paper towels and slice into rings.

2 Rinse the spinach and leave wet (so it won't stick to the wok). Heat the wok until very hot, add the spinach and toss over high heat until wilted. Transfer to a serving plate.

3 Heat the wok until very hot, add 1 tablespoon of the oil and swirl it around to coat the side. Stir-fry the squid rings, prawns and scallops in batches over high heat until they turn opaque and are cooked through. Remove all of the seafood from the wok and set aside. Heat 1 tablespoon of the oil and cook the garlic and chilli for 1–2 minutes, or until softened.

4 Add the plum sauce, brown sugar and lime juice to the wok. Bring to the boil, then reduce the heat and simmer for 4–5 minutes, or until the sauce thickens. Return the squid rings, prawns and scallops to the wok, add the sliced spring onion and toss to coat in the sauce. Serve the seafood on top of the stir-fried spinach.

Peel the prawns and remove the dark veins from their backs.

Cut the hard white muscle and any dark veins from the scallops.

NUTRITION PER SERVE
Protein 65 g; Fat 4 g; Carbohydrate 20 g; Dietary Fibre 7.5 g; Cholesterol 470 mg; 1605 kJ (385 Cal)

Black fungus with prawns

PREPARATION TIME: 25 MINUTES | TOTAL COOKING TIME: 8 MINUTES | SERVES 4

20 g (¾ oz) dried black fungus

2 teaspoons cornflour (cornstarch)

60 ml (2 fl oz/¼ cup) mirin

1 tablespoon rice wine vinegar

1 tablespoon soy sauce

1–2 small red chillies, seeded and
    finely chopped

1–2 garlic cloves, crushed

2 teaspoons grated fresh ginger

1 tablespoon oil

500 g (1 lb 2 oz) raw prawns (shrimp), peeled,
    deveined and halved lengthways

½ red capsicum (pepper), cut into matchsticks

1 celery stalk, cut into matchsticks

1 carrot, cut into matchsticks

4 spring onions (scallions), cut into short
    pieces and sliced lengthways

230 g (8 oz) tin water chestnuts, drained

1 Place the black fungus in a bowl and cover with boiling water. Leave until doubled in volume and softened. Drain, squeeze dry and chop roughly.

2 Mix the cornflour with 60 ml (2 fl oz/¼ cup) water in a bowl until smooth. Add the mirin, vinegar, soy sauce, chilli, garlic and ginger.

3 Heat the wok until very hot, add the oil and swirl it around to coat the side. Stir-fry the prawns briefly until they are just starting to change colour. Add the capsicum, celery, carrot, spring onion, water chestnuts and black fungus and stir-fry over medium–high heat for 2–3 minutes, or until tender. Remove from the wok.

4 Add the cornflour mixture to the wok and stir until the mixture boils and thickens. Stir in the prawns and vegetables. Serve at once.

NUTRITION PER SERVE
Protein 30 g; Fat 6.5 g; Carbohydrate 30 g; Dietary Fibre 5 g; Cholesterol 185 mg; 1205 kJ (290 Cal)

Peel the prawns, removing the large veins from their backs, then cut them down the middle.

Put the black fungus in a bowl and cover with boiling water.

Crab with asparagus and broccoli

PREPARATION TIME: 30 MINUTES | TOTAL COOKING TIME: 15 MINUTES | SERVES 4

250 g (9 oz) thick dried rice stick noodles
oil, for cooking
3 lemongrass stems, white part only, very
    thinly sliced
1 tablespoon grated fresh ginger
4 spring onions (scallions), chopped
¼ teaspoon green peppercorns in
    brine, drained and crushed
750 g (1 lb 10 oz) broccoli, cut into
    small florets
150 g (5½ oz) asparagus, cut into
    short lengths
3 teaspoons sesame oil
1 teaspoon sugar
250 g (9 oz) cooked fresh crabmeat
    (see HINT)
70 g (2½ oz) garlic chives, snipped
2 tablespoons lemon juice

1 Soak the noodles in boiling water for 8 minutes, or until soft and tender. Drain, cool a little, then drizzle with ½ tablespoon of oil and mix in lightly with your fingertips to prevent them from sticking together. Cover to keep warm.

2 Heat the wok until very hot, add 1 tablespoon of the oil and swirl it around to coat the side. Stir-fry the lemongrass, ginger and spring onion for 15 seconds. Add the peppercorns, broccoli and asparagus and stir-fry for 1 minute. Add the sesame oil and sugar, and cook, covered, for 1–2 minutes, or until the asparagus and broccoli are just tender. Add the crabmeat and cook for 1–2 minutes, or until heated through.

3 Add the noodles, chives and lemon juice, and toss well. Season well with salt and pepper. Serve immediately.

HINT: *Good fishmongers sell fresh crabmeat in vacuum packets. Alternatively, you can use the meat from 2 very fresh cooked blue swimmer crabs. Tinned crabmeat can also be used.*

NUTRITION PER SERVE
Protein 15 g; Fat 15 g; Carbohydrate 55 g; Dietary Fibre 2.5 g; Cholesterol 50 mg; 1705 kJ (405 Cal)

Slice the lemongrass very thinly, using only the white part of the stem.

Cover the noodles with boiling water and leave for 8 minutes, until they have softened.

Stir-fry the lemongrass, ginger and spring onion quickly, before adding the vegetables.

Mussels with lemongrass, basil and wine

PREPARATION TIME: 30 MINUTES | TOTAL COOKING TIME: 15 MINUTES | SERVES 4–6

1 kg (2 lb 4 oz) black mussels
1 tablespoon oil
1 onion, chopped
4 garlic cloves, chopped
2 lemongrass stems, white part only, chopped
1–2 teaspoons chopped small red chillies
250 ml (9 fl oz/1 cup) white wine
1 tablespoon fish sauce
1 large handful Thai basil leaves

1 Scrub the mussels and debeard. Soak them in a bowl of cold water for 10 minutes; drain and discard any broken mussels, or open ones that don't close when tapped on the work surface.

2 Heat the oil in a wok and stir-fry the onion, garlic, lemongrass and chilli over low heat for 4 minutes. Add the wine and fish sauce and cook for 3 minutes.

3 Add the mussels to the wok and toss well. Cover the wok, increase the heat and cook for 3–4 minutes, or until the mussels open. When cooked, discard any unopened mussels. Add the basil and toss well before serving.

HINT: *Do not overcook the mussels or they will become tough. Use small fresh black mussels and buy a few extra, in case any are cracked, damaged or fail to open when cooked.*

After scrubbing the mussels with a brush, pull the beards off and discard.

Add the wine and fish sauce to the wok and cook for 3 minutes.

NUTRITION PER SERVE (6)
Protein 13 g; Fat 5 g; Carbohydrate 1.5 g; Dietary Fibre 0 g; Cholesterol 30 mg; 1271 kJ (302 Cal)

Prawns and scallops with Thai spices

PREPARATION TIME: 25 MINUTES + 30 MINUTES REFRIGERATION | TOTAL COOKING TIME: 10 MINUTES | SERVES 4

500 g (1 lb 2 oz) raw prawns (shrimp), peeled
 and deveined, tails intact
250 g (9 oz) scallops
1–2 tablespoons red curry paste, to taste
2 tablespoons oil
2 ripe tomatoes, chopped
2 tablespoons lime juice
2 teaspoons finely grated lime zest

1   Combine the prawns, scallops, curry paste and oil in a bowl; cover and refrigerate for about 30 minutes.

2   Heat a wok until it is very hot. Toss the seafood in the curry paste again to coat well and add to the wok in 2–3 batches. Cook each batch for 3 minutes, tossing frequently.

3   Remove from the heat and return all the seafood to the wok. Add the tomato and lime juice and stir well. Serve immediately, garnished with lime zest.

HINT: *Cook seafood quickly in a hot wok to seal in the juices and flavour. Don't overcook seafood or it will become tough.*

NUTRITION PER SERVE
Protein 33 g; Fat 11 g; Carbohydrate 2 g; Dietary Fibre 0.5 g; Cholesterol 205 mg; 1020 kJ (245 Cal)

Place the prawns, scallops, oil and curry paste in a bowl and toss to combine well.

Toss the seafood in a hot wok, in batches, for 3 minutes each batch.

Add the chopped tomatoes and lime juice to the seafood and toss to combine.

Balinese chilli squid

PREPARATION TIME: 30 MINUTES | TOTAL COOKING TIME: 15 MINUTES | SERVES 4

750 g (1 lb 10 oz) squid tubes
60 ml (2 fl oz/¼ cup) lime juice
3 tablespoons vegetable oil
1 large red chilli, seeded and sliced
3 spring onions (scallions), sliced, plus extra
  finely shredded spring onion, to garnish
1 tablespoon tamarind concentrate
1 lemongrass stem, white part only,
  finely sliced
250 ml (9 fl oz/1 cup) chicken stock
5 Thai basil leaves, shredded

SPICE PASTE
2 large red chillies, seeded and chopped
2 garlic cloves, chopped
2 cm (¾ inch) piece fresh ginger, chopped
2 cm (¾ inch) piece fresh turmeric, chopped
3 spring onions (scallions), chopped
1 tomato, peeled, seeded and chopped
2 teaspoons coriander seeds
1 teaspoon shrimp paste

1 Score the underside flesh of the squid in a fine criss-cross pattern and cut into large pieces. Place in a bowl with the lime juice and season well.

2 To make the spice paste, grind the chilli, garlic, ginger, turmeric, spring onion, tomato, coriander seeds and shrimp paste in a food processor.

3 Heat 2 tablespoons of the oil in a wok. Cook the squid, chilli and spring onion in batches for 2 minutes over high heat—don't overcook the squid. Remove from the wok.

4 Heat the remaining oil and add the spice paste, tamarind concentrate and lemongrass. Cook, stirring, over medium heat for 5 minutes.

5 Return the squid to the wok and add the stock. Season with pepper and add the basil. Bring to the boil, then reduce the heat and simmer for 2 minutes. Serve immediately, garnished with the extra spring onion.

NUTRITION PER SERVE
Protein 35 g; Fat 15 g; Carbohydrate 3 g; Dietary Fibre 2 g; Cholesterol 375 mg; 1245 kJ (295 Cal)

Score the underside flesh of the squid and cut into large pieces.

After adding the lime juice, season the squid pieces well with salt and pepper.

Vietnamese prawns with snake beans

PREPARATION TIME: 25 MINUTES | TOTAL COOKING TIME: 15 MINUTES | SERVES 4

2 tablespoons oil
2 onions, very finely sliced
5 garlic cloves, finely chopped
2 lemongrass stems, white part only, very
    finely sliced
3 red chillies, seeded and finely sliced
250 g (9 oz) snake beans, topped and tailed
    and cut into short pieces (see HINT)
300 g (10½ oz) raw prawns (shrimp), peeled
    and deveined
2 teaspoons sugar
1 tablespoon fish sauce
1 tablespoon rice wine vinegar
garlic chives, to garnish

1   Heat the oil in a large wok. Add the onion, garlic, lemongrass and chilli and stir-fry over medium–high heat for 4 minutes, or until soft and golden.

2   Add the beans to the wok and stir-fry for 2–3 minutes, or until bright green. Add the prawns and sugar and toss gently for 3 minutes.

3   Add the fish sauce and rice wine vinegar, toss well and serve, sprinkled with garlic chives.

HINT: *Snake beans are dark green beans, about 30 cm (12 inches) long, with pointed tips. They are sold at speciality fruit and vegetable and Asian food stores. If they are not available, green beans can be used.*

Top and tail the snake beans and then cut them into short pieces.

Stir-fry the onion, garlic, lemongrass and chilli in the wok.

NUTRITION PER SERVE
Protein 18 g; Fat 10 g; Carbohydrate 4 g; Dietary
Fibre 2.5 g; Cholesterol 112 mg; 765 kJ (183 Cal)

Marinated chilli squid

PREPARATION TIME: 10 MINUTES + 2–3 HOURS MARINATING | TOTAL COOKING TIME: 15 MINUTES | SERVES 4

500 g (1 lb 2 oz) squid tubes
1 tablespoon finely chopped fresh ginger
2–3 teaspoons finely chopped red chilli
3 garlic cloves, finely chopped
60 ml (2 fl oz/¼ cup) oil
2 onions, thinly sliced
500 g (1 lb 2 oz) baby bok choy (pak choy),
    roughly chopped

1   Wash the squid well and dry with paper towels. Cut into 1 cm (½ inch) rings and place in a bowl with the ginger, chilli, garlic and oil. Toss well. Cover and refrigerate for 2–3 hours.

2   Heat the wok until very hot and stir-fry the squid rings over high heat in three batches for 1–2 minutes, reserving the marinade. Remove from the wok as soon as the squid turns white. Keep the wok very hot and don't cook the squid for too long or it will toughen. Remove all the squid from the wok.

3   Pour the reserved marinade into the wok and bring to the boil. Add the onion and cook over medium heat for 3–4 minutes, or until slightly softened. Add the bok choy, cover and steam for 2 minutes, or until wilted. Add the squid and toss. Serve immediately.

NUTRITION PER SERVE
Protein 25 g; Fat 15 g; Carbohydrate 7 g; Dietary Fibre 2 g; Cholesterol 250 mg; 1105 kJ (265 Cal)

Wash the squid tubes well and pat them dry with paper towels.

Using a sharp knife, slice the washed squid tubes into rings.

Remove the squid from the wok as soon as it turns white, or it will be rubbery.

Ginger garlic prawn salad

PREPARATION TIME: 35 MINUTES | TOTAL COOKING TIME: 15 MINUTES | SERVES 4

oil, for cooking
5 garlic cloves, finely chopped
1 tablespoon grated fresh ginger
1 onion, sliced
500 g (1 lb 2 oz) raw prawns (shrimp), peeled
  and deveined, tails intact
1 carrot, cut into matchsticks
2 celery stalks, cut into matchsticks
100 g (3½ oz) snow peas (mangetouts), sliced
100 g (3½ oz) green beans, cut into
  short lengths
2 teaspoons cornflour (cornstarch)
60 ml (2 fl oz/¼ cup) vegetable stock
2 tablespoons soy sauce
2 teaspoons soft brown sugar
500 g (1 lb 2 oz) watercress
40 g (1½ oz/¼ cup) roasted unsalted peanuts,
  roughly chopped

1   Heat the wok until very hot, add
1 tablespoon of the oil and swirl it around
to coat the side. Stir-fry the garlic, ginger, onion
and prawns over high heat for 5 minutes, or
until the prawns have turned pink and are
cooked. Remove from the wok.

2   Reheat the wok, add 1 tablespoon of the
oil and stir-fry the carrot, celery, snow peas
and beans over high heat for 3–4 minutes. Mix
the cornflour with a little of the stock to form
a paste. Mix in the remaining stock, soy sauce
and sugar. Pour into the wok and stir until the
sauce boils and thickens.

3   Return the prawns to the wok, stirring for
1–2 minutes, or until heated through. Serve on
a bed of watercress, and sprinkle the chopped
peanuts over the top.

NUTRITION PER SERVE
Protein 35 g; Fat 15 g; Carbohydrate 15 g; Dietary
Fibre 10 g; Cholesterol 185 mg; 1450 kJ (350 Cal)

Peel the heads and shells from the prawns, leaving the tails intact.

Remove the dark veins from the prawns by pulling them out with your fingers.

Cut the celery stalks into pieces and then into matchsticks for quick and even cooking.

Sweet chilli squid

PREPARATION TIME: 20 MINUTES | TOTAL COOKING TIME: 10 MINUTES | SERVES 4

750 g (1 lb 10 oz) squid tubes
1 tablespoon peanut oil
1 tablespoon finely grated fresh ginger
2 garlic cloves, crushed
8 spring onions (scallions), chopped
2 tablespoons sweet chilli sauce
2 tablespoons Chinese barbecue sauce
1 tablespoon soy sauce
550 g (1 lb 4 oz/1 bunch) bok choy
    (pak choy), cut into short pieces
1 tablespoon chopped coriander
    (cilantro) leaves

1   Cut the squid tubes open, score diagonal slashes across the inside surface and cut into strips.

2   Heat a wok until very hot, add the oil and swirl to coat. Add the ginger, garlic, spring onion and squid and stir-fry for 3 minutes, or until browned.

3   Add the sauces and 2 tablespoons water to the wok and stir-fry for 2 minutes, or until the squid is just tender. Add the bok choy and coriander, and stir-fry for 1 minute, or until the bok choy is tender.

NUTRITION PER SERVE
Protein 40 g; Fat 8 g; Carbohydrate 4 g; Dietary Fibre 7.5 g; Cholesterol 375 mg; 1030 kJ (245 Cal)

Rinse the bok choy thoroughly, then cut it into short pieces.

Score diagonal slashes across the inside surface of the squid tubes, then cut into strips.

Stir-fry the squid for 3 minutes. The score marks in the flesh will make it curl nicely.

Lemongrass prawns

PREPARATION TIME: 30 MINUTES | TOTAL COOKING TIME: 10 MINUTES | SERVES 4

1 tablespoon peanut oil

2 garlic cloves, crushed

1 tablespoon finely grated fresh ginger

2 tablespoons finely chopped lemongrass,
    white part only

8 spring onions (scallions), cut into short
    lengths, plus extra finely shredded spring
    onion, to garnish

1 kg (2 lb 4 oz) raw prawns (shrimp), peeled,
    deveined, tails intact

2 tablespoons lime juice

1 tablespoon soft brown sugar

2 teaspoons fish sauce

60 ml (2 fl oz/¼ cup) chicken stock

1 teaspoon cornflour (cornstarch)

500 g (1 lb 2 oz) baby bok choy
    (pak choy), cut in half lengthways

1 very large handful mint, chopped

1   Heat a wok until very hot, add the oil and swirl to coat. Add the garlic, ginger, lemongrass and spring onion, and stir-fry for 1 minute, or until fragrant. Add the prawns and stir-fry for 2 minutes.

2   Place the lime juice, sugar, fish sauce, chicken stock and cornflour in a small bowl. Mix well, then add to the wok and stir until the sauce boils and thickens. Cook for a further 1–2 minutes, or until the prawns are pink and just tender.

3   Add the bok choy and stir-fry for 1 minute, or until wilted. Stir in the mint, garnish with the spring onion and serve.

Peel the prawn bodies, remove the heads and dark veins, but leave the tail shells on.

Rinse the bok choy thoroughly and then slice in half down the middle.

NUTRITION PER SERVE
Protein 60 g; Fat 8.5 g; Carbohydrate 8 g; Dietary Fibre 1.6 g; Cholesterol 373 mg; 1433 kJ (342 Cal)

Tofu and tempeh

Crisp tofu in hot bean sauce

PREPARATION TIME: 35 MINUTES + 30 MINUTES MARINATING | TOTAL COOKING TIME: 15 MINUTES | SERVES 4

500 g (1 lb 2 oz) firm tofu, cut into
    small cubes
2 tablespoons peanut oil
60 ml (2 fl oz/¼ cup) soy sauce
2 teaspoons finely grated fresh ginger
130 g (4½ oz/¾ cup) rice flour
oil, for cooking
2 onions, cut into thin wedges
2 garlic cloves, finely chopped
2 teaspoons soft brown sugar
½ red capsicum (pepper), cut into short,
    thin strips
5 spring onions (scallions), cut into
    short pieces, plus extra finely shredded
    spring onion, to garnish
2 tablespoons dry sherry
2 teaspoons finely grated orange zest
2 tablespoons hot bean paste

1 Place the tofu in a glass or ceramic bowl with the peanut oil. Add the soy sauce and ginger, cover and refrigerate for 30 minutes.

2 Drain the tofu, reserving the marinade, and toss several pieces at a time in the rice flour to coat heavily. Heat the wok until very hot, add about 60 ml (2 fl oz/¼ cup) of the oil and swirl it around to coat the side. Add half the tofu to the hot oil and stir-fry over medium heat for 1½ minutes, or until golden all over. Remove from the wok and drain on paper towels. Repeat with the remaining tofu. Keep warm. Drain excess oil from the wok.

3 Reheat the wok and stir-fry the onion, garlic and sugar for 3 minutes, or until golden. Add the capsicum, spring onion, sherry, orange zest, bean paste and the reserved tofu marinade. Stir and bring to the boil. Return the tofu to the wok, toss to heat through and serve, garnished with shredded spring onion.

NUTRITION PER SERVE
Protein 15 g; Fat 8 g; Carbohydrate 40 g; Dietary
Fibre 3 g; Cholesterol 0 mg; 1215 kJ (290 Cal)

Place the tofu in a bowl with the peanut oil and add the soy sauce.

Drain the tofu in a sieve, then toss it in the rice flour to coat heavily.

Stir-fry the tofu until it is golden on all sides, then drain on paper towels.

Chilli tempeh

PREPARATION TIME: 15 MINUTES | TOTAL COOKING TIME: 10 MINUTES | SERVES 4

250 g (9 oz) tempeh
oil, for cooking
1 onion, thinly sliced
150 g (5½ oz/1 bunch) asparagus, cut into
    short lengths
1 large carrot, cut into thick matchsticks
125 g (4½ oz) snow peas (mangetouts),
    chopped
425 g (15 oz) tin baby corn, drained
2 tablespoons sweet chilli sauce
2 tablespoons kecap manis (see NOTE,
    page 18)
2 tablespoons dry sherry

1 Drain the tempeh, pat dry with paper towels and cut into bite-sized pieces for stir-frying.

2 Heat the wok until very hot, add 2 tablespoons of the oil and swirl it around to coat the side. Stir-fry the tempeh in batches until crisp. Remove from the wok and set aside.

3 Reheat the wok, add a little more oil if necessary and stir-fry the onion for 1 minute. Add the asparagus, carrot and snow peas, and stir-fry for 2–3 minutes, or until the vegetables are just tender.

4 Return the fried tempeh to the wok and add the baby corn, sweet chilli sauce, kecap manis and sherry. Bring to the boil, then reduce the heat and simmer for 2 minutes. Toss well until heated through and serve.

Peel the carrot, cut it into short lengths and then into thick matchsticks.

Drain the tempeh, dry it on paper towels and cut it into bite-sized pieces.

NUTRITION PER SERVE
Protein 5 g; Fat 15 g; Carbohydrate 10 g; Dietary
Fibre 8 g; Cholesterol 0 mg; 1270 kJ (300 Cal)

Deep-fried tofu with hokkien noodles

PREPARATION TIME: **10** MINUTES | TOTAL COOKING TIME: **5** MINUTES | SERVES **4**

100 g (3½ oz) deep-fried tofu puffs
    (see HINT)
2 tablespoons oil
1 onion, sliced
1 red capsicum (pepper), cut into squares
3 garlic cloves, crushed
2 teaspoons grated fresh ginger
120 g (4¼ oz/¾ cup) small chunks
    fresh pineapple
500 g (1 lb 2 oz) thin hokkien (egg) noodles,
    gently pulled apart
60 ml (2 fl oz/¼ cup) pineapple juice
60 ml (2 fl oz/¼ cup) hoisin sauce
1 very large handful fresh coriander (cilantro),
    roughly chopped, plus extra leaves,
    to garnish

1 Slice the tofu puffs into three, then cut each slice into two or three pieces.

2 Heat the wok until very hot, add the oil and stir-fry the onion and capsicum for 1–2 minutes, or until beginning to soften. Add the garlic and ginger, stir-fry for 1 minute, then add the tofu and stir-fry for 2 minutes.

3 Add the pineapple chunks and noodles and toss until the mixture is combined and heated through. Add the pineapple juice, hoisin sauce and chopped coriander and toss to combine. Serve immediately garnished with extra coriander leaves.

HINT: *Deep-fried tofu puffs are available from the refrigerated section in Asian grocery stores and some supermarkets. They have a very different texture to ordinary tofu.*

NUTRITION PER SERVE
Protein 10 g; Fat 15 g; Carbohydrate 65 g; Dietary
Fibre 3.5 g; Cholesterol 0 mg; 1830 kJ (435 Cal)

Use your fingers to gently separate the hokkien noodles before cooking.

Slice the tofu puffs into three, then cut into smaller pieces.

Honey-braised vegetables with bean curd

PREPARATION TIME: 30 MINUTES + 30 MINUTES SOAKING | COOKING TIME: 20 MINUTES | SERVES 6

8 dried Chinese mushrooms
20 dried lily buds (see HINT)
2 tablespoons peanut oil
3 thin slices fresh ginger, cut into strips
250 g (9 oz) white sweet potato, halved
    and sliced
2 tablespoons soy sauce
1 tablespoon honey
2 teaspoons sesame oil
60 g (2¼ oz) deep-fried tofu puffs, cut
    into thin strips
2 teaspoons cornflour (cornstarch)
4 spring onions (scallions), cut into
    short lengths, plus extra finely shredded
    spring onion, to garnish
410 g (14½ oz) tin baby corn, drained
225 g (8 oz) tin water chestnuts, drained

1 Soak the mushrooms in hot water for 30 minutes. Drain, reserving 185 ml (6 fl oz/ ¾ cup) of the liquid. Squeeze dry with your hands. Remove the stems and slice the mushrooms thinly. Soak the lily buds separately in warm water for 30 minutes, then drain.

2 Heat the oil in a wok. Add the ginger and stir-fry for 1 minute. Add the mushrooms and lily buds and stir-fry for 30 seconds. Add the sweet potato with the soy sauce, honey, sesame oil, mushroom liquid and tofu. Simmer in the wok for 15 minutes.

3 Dissolve the cornflour in a little water and add to the wok. Stir until the liquid thickens. Add the spring onion, corn and water chestnuts and toss to heat through before serving. Garnish with the shredded spring onion.

HINT: *Dried lily buds are a Chinese speciality. They can be left out of the recipe without altering the flavour greatly.*

NUTRITION PER SERVE
Protein 4 g; Fat 10 g; Carbohydrate 30 g; Dietary Fibre 5 g; Cholesterol 0 mg; 920 kJ (220 Cal)

Cut three thin slices of fresh ginger and then cut the slices into thin strips.

Add the sweet potato, soy sauce, honey, sesame oil, mushroom liquid and tofu to the wok.

Stir until the sauce thickens, then add the spring onion, corn and water chestnuts.

Chinese tofu

PREPARATION TIME: 20 MINUTES | TOTAL COOKING TIME: 20 MINUTES | SERVES 4–6

125 g (4½ oz) rice vermicelli
oil, for cooking
1 tablespoon soy sauce
1 tablespoon sherry
1 tablespoon oyster sauce
125 ml (4 fl oz/½ cup) chicken stock
2 teaspoons cornflour (cornstarch)
1 garlic clove, crushed
1 teaspoon grated fresh ginger
375 g (13 oz) firm tofu, cut into small pieces
2 carrots, cut into matchsticks
250 g (9 oz) snow peas (mangetouts), trimmed
4 spring onions (scallions), finely sliced
425 g (15 oz) tin straw mushrooms, drained

1   Break the vermicelli into short lengths. Heat 4 tablespoons of the oil in a wok. Cook the vermicelli in batches over medium heat until crisp, adding more oil when necessary. Drain on paper towels.

2   Combine the soy sauce, sherry, oyster sauce and chicken stock. Blend the cornflour with 2 teaspoons water.

3   Reheat the wok and heat a tablespoon of oil. Add the garlic and ginger and cook over high heat for 1 minute. Add the tofu and stir-fry for 3 minutes. Remove from the wok. Add the carrot and snow peas and stir-fry for 1 minute. Add the sauce and stock mixture, cover and cook for another 3 minutes or until the vegetables are just tender. Add the tofu.

4   Add the spring onion, mushrooms and blended cornflour. Stir until the sauce has thickened, then serve with the rice vermicelli.

Fry the vermicelli in hot oil and then drain on paper towels.

Combine the soy sauce, sherry, oyster sauce and chicken stock.

NUTRITION PER SERVE (6)
Protein 15 g; Fat 35 g; Carbohydrate 11 g; Dietary Fibre 6 g; Cholesterol 0 mg; 1418 kJ (338 Cal)

Tofu and peanut noodles

PREPARATION TIME: 10 MINUTES | TOTAL COOKING TIME: 10 MINUTES | SERVES 4

250 g (9 oz) firm tofu, cut into small pieces
2 garlic cloves, crushed
1 teaspoon grated fresh ginger
80 ml (2½ fl oz/⅓ cup) kecap manis
    (see NOTE, page 18)
90 g (3¼ oz/⅓ cup) peanut butter
2 tablespoons peanut or vegetable oil
500 g (1 lb 2 oz) hokkien (egg) noodles
1 onion, chopped
1 red capsicum (pepper), chopped
125 g (4½ oz) broccoli, cut into small florets

1 Combine the tofu with the garlic, ginger and half the kecap manis in a small bowl. Place the peanut butter, 125 ml (4 fl oz/½ cup) water and the remaining kecap manis in another bowl and mix well.

2 Heat the oil in a large wok. Drain the tofu and reserve the marinade. Cook the tofu in two batches in the hot oil until well browned. Remove from the wok.

3 Place the noodles in a large heatproof bowl. Cover with boiling water and leave for 2 minutes. Drain and gently pull the noodles apart.

4 Add the vegetables to the wok and stir-fry until just tender. Add the tofu, reserved marinade and noodles. Add the peanut butter mixture and toss until heated through.

NUTRITION PER SERVE
Protein 32 g; Fat 30 g; Carbohydrate 96 g; Dietary
Fibre 8 g; Cholesterol 20 mg; 3140 kJ (697 Cal)

Mix together the tofu, garlic, ginger and half the kecap manis in a bowl.

Cook the tofu in two batches in the hot oil until it is well browned.

Vegetarian phad thai

PREPARATION TIME: 20 MINUTES | TOTAL COOKING TIME: 15 MINUTES | SERVES 4

400 g (14 oz) flat rice-stick noodles

2 tablespoons peanut oil

2 eggs, lightly beaten

1 onion, cut into thin wedges

2 garlic cloves, crushed

1 small red capsicum (pepper), cut into thin strips

100 g (3½ oz) deep-fried tofu puffs, thinly sliced

6 spring onions (scallions), thinly sliced on the diagonal

2 very large handfuls coriander (cilantro) leaves, chopped

60 ml (2 fl oz/¼ cup) soy sauce

2 tablespoons lime juice

1 tablespoon soft brown sugar

2 teaspoons sambal oelek (South-East Asian chilli paste)

90 g (3¼ oz/1 cup) bean sprouts

40 g (1½ oz/¼ cup) chopped roasted unsalted peanuts

1 Cook the noodles in a saucepan of boiling water for 5–10 minutes, or until tender. Drain and set aside.

2 Heat a wok over high heat and add enough peanut oil to coat the bottom and side. When smoking, add the egg and swirl to form a thin omelette. Cook for 30 seconds, or until just set. Roll up, remove and thinly slice.

3 Heat the remaining oil in the wok. Add the onion, garlic and capsicum and cook over high heat for 2–3 minutes, or until the onion softens. Add the noodles, tossing well. Stir in the omelette, tofu, spring onion and half the coriander.

4 Pour in the combined soy sauce, lime juice, sugar and sambal oelek and toss well. Sprinkle with the bean sprouts and top with roasted peanuts and the remaining coriander to serve.

NUTRITION PER SERVE
Protein 13 g; Fat 21 g; Carbohydrate 34 g; Dietary Fibre 5 g; Cholesterol 90 mg; 1565 kJ (375 Cal)

Using a sharp knife, slice the deep-fried tofu puffs into thin strips.

Once the omelette is golden and set, carefully roll it up, remove from the wok and thinly slice.

Stir in the omelette, tofu, spring onion and half of the coriander.

Asian greens with teriyaki tofu dressing

PREPARATION TIME: 15 MINUTES I TOTAL COOKING TIME: 20 MINUTES I SERVES 6

650 g (1 lb 7 oz) baby bok choy (pak choy)
500 g (1 lb 2 oz) choy sum
440 g (15½ oz) snake beans, topped and tailed
60 ml (2 fl oz/¼ cup) oil
1 onion, thinly sliced
60 g (2¼ oz/⅓ cup) soft brown sugar
½ teaspoon ground chilli
2 tablespoons grated fresh ginger
250 ml (9 fl oz/1 cup) teriyaki sauce
1 tablespoon sesame oil
600 g (1 lb 5 oz) silken firm tofu, drained

1   Cut the the baby bok choy and choy sum widthways into thirds. Chop the snake beans into shorter lengths.

2   Heat a wok over high heat, add 1 tablespoon of the oil and swirl to coat the side. Cook the onion for 3–5 minutes, or until crisp. Remove with a slotted spoon and drain on paper towels.

3   Heat 1 tablespoon of the oil in the wok, add half the greens and stir-fry for 2–3 minutes, or until wilted. Remove and keep warm. Repeat with the remaining oil and greens. Remove. Drain any liquid from the wok.

4   Add the combined sugar, chilli, ginger and teriyaki sauce to the wok and bring to the boil. Simmer for 1 minute. Add the sesame oil and tofu and simmer for 2 minutes, turning once—the tofu will break up. Divide the greens among serving plates, then top with the dressing. Sprinkle with the fried onion to serve.

Cut the baby bok choy and choy sum widthways into thirds.

Turn the tofu with a spatula halfway through the cooking time.

NUTRITION PER SERVE
Protein 19 g; Fat 11 g; Carbohydrate 20 g; Dietary Fibre 11 g; Cholesterol 1 mg; 1093 kJ (260 Cal)

Fried tofu, choy sum and baby corn in oyster sauce

PREPARATION TIME: 5 MINUTES | TOTAL COOKING TIME: 6 MINUTES | SERVES 4

2 tablespoons peanut oil
400 g (14 oz) deep-fried tofu puffs, halved
4 tablespoons oyster sauce
2 tablespoons light soy sauce
2 tablespoons sweet chilli sauce
2 tablespoons honey
2 garlic cloves, crushed
12 baby corn, halved lengthways
500 g (1 lb 2 oz) choy sum leaves, cut into
    short lengths

1 Heat a wok over high heat, add the oil and swirl to coat the side. Add the tofu puffs and stir-fry for 2 minutes, or until crisp and golden.

2 Place the oyster sauce, soy sauce, sweet chilli sauce and honey in a small bowl and mix together well.

3 Add the garlic, baby corn and choy sum to the wok and pour in the combined sauce, along with 60 ml (2 fl oz/¼ cup) water. Stir-fry for 3–4 minutes, or until the leaves have just wilted. Serve immediately.

NUTRITION PER SERVE
Protein 12 g; Fat 22 g; Carbohydrate 45 g; Dietary
Fibre 8 g; Cholesterol 0 mg; 1975 kJ (470 Cal)

Stir-fry the tofu puffs for 2 minutes, or until crispy and golden.

Place the sauces and honey in a small bowl and mix together well.

Add the garlic, baby corn and choy sum to the wok and stir-fry.

Tofu with shoshoyu and mirin

PREPARATION TIME: 20 MINUTES + 2 HOURS MARINATING | TOTAL COOKING TIME: 20 MINUTES | SERVES 4

500 g (1 lb 2 oz) firm tofu (see HINT), cut into small cubes
80 ml (2½ fl oz/⅓ cup) Japanese soy sauce
60 ml (2 fl oz/¼ cup) mirin
3 garlic cloves, finely chopped
2 tablespoons finely chopped fresh ginger
oil, for cooking
1 onion, thinly sliced
2 carrots, cut into batons
1 red capsicum (pepper), thinly sliced
150 g (5½ oz) snow peas (mangetouts), thinly sliced

1 Combine the tofu with the soy sauce, mirin, garlic and ginger in a glass or ceramic bowl. Cover and refrigerate for 2 hours.

2 Heat the wok until very hot, add 1 tablespoon of the oil and swirl it around to coat the side. Drain the tofu, reserving the marinade. Stir-fry the tofu in three batches over high heat until it is golden brown. Heat 1 tablespoon of the oil between batches. Remove all the tofu from the wok and drain on paper towels.

3 Reheat the wok, add 1 tablespoon of the oil and stir-fry the onion, carrot and capsicum over medium–high heat for 3–4 minutes, or until the vegetables are tender. Add the snow peas and cook for 3 minutes.

4 Increase the heat to high and add the reserved marinade, tossing the vegetables in the marinade until they are thoroughly coated and the sauce boils. Return the tofu to the wok and toss until the mixture is well combined and the tofu is heated through. Season well with salt and pepper, and serve immediately.

NUTRITION PER SERVE
Protein 15 g; Fat 15 g; Carbohydrate 9 g; Dietary Fibre 4 g; Cholesterol 0 mg; 930 kJ (220 Cal)

HINT: *Tofu does not have a strong flavour of its own but takes on flavour from whatever it is mixed with. Choose the firmest tofu you can find for this recipe. Tempeh could also be used.*

Buy the firmest tofu you can find, drain it and cut into bite-sized cubes.

Combine the tofu, soy sauce, mirin, garlic and ginger in a bowl and leave to marinate.

Tempeh with Chinese greens

PREPARATION TIME: 15 MINUTES | TOTAL COOKING TIME: 15 MINUTES | SERVES 4

1 teaspoon sesame oil
1 tablespoon peanut oil
2 garlic cloves, crushed
1 tablespoon grated fresh ginger
1 red chilli, finely sliced
4 spring onions (scallions), sliced on
    the diagonal
300 g (10½ oz) tempeh, cut into small cubes
500 g (1 lb 2 oz) baby bok choy
    (pak choy) leaves
800 g (1 lb 12 oz) Chinese broccoli, chopped
125 ml (4 fl oz/½ cup) mushroom oyster sauce
2 tablespoons rice vinegar
2 tablespoons coriander (cilantro) leaves
40 g (1½ oz/¼ cup) toasted cashew nuts

1　Heat the oils in a wok over high heat, add the garlic, ginger, chilli and spring onion and cook for 1–2 minutes, or until the onion is soft. Add the tempeh and cook for 5 minutes, or until golden. Remove from the wok and keep warm.

2　Add half the greens and 1 tablespoon water to the wok and cook, covered, for 3–4 minutes, or until wilted. Remove and repeat with the remaining greens and more water.

3　Return the greens and tempeh to the wok, add the sauce and vinegar and warm through. Top with the coriander and nuts to serve.

Stir-fry the garlic, ginger, chilli and spring onion for 1–2 minutes.

Add the tempeh and stir-fry for 5 minutes, or until it has turned golden.

NUTRITION PER SERVE
Protein 23 g; Fat 15 g; Carbohydrate 12 g; Dietary Fibre 15 g; Cholesterol 0 mg; 2220 kJ (529 Cal)

Tofu with bok choy

PREPARATION TIME: 20 MINUTES + 10 MINUTES MARINATING | TOTAL COOKING TIME: 10 MINUTES | SERVES 4

600 g (1 lb 5 oz) firm tofu, cut into
     small pieces
1 tablespoon grated fresh ginger
2 tablespoons soy sauce
2 tablespoons peanut oil
1 red onion, finely sliced
4 garlic cloves, crushed
500 g (1 lb 2 oz) baby bok choy (pak choy),
     sliced lengthways
2 teaspoons sesame oil
2 tablespoons kecap manis (see NOTE,
     page 18)
60 ml (2 fl oz/¼ cup) sweet chilli sauce
1 tablespoon toasted sesame seeds

1   Put the tofu in a bowl with the ginger.
Pour in the soy sauce and leave to marinate
for 10 minutes. Drain.

2   Heat a wok until very hot, add half the
peanut oil and swirl to coat the base and side of
the wok. When the oil is hot, add the onion and
stir-fry for 3 minutes, or until soft. Add the tofu
and garlic and stir-fry for 3 minutes, or until the
tofu is golden. Remove and keep warm.

3   Reheat the wok until very hot, add the
remaining peanut oil and swirl to coat. Add
the bok choy and stir-fry for 2 minutes, or until
wilted. Return the tofu mixture to the wok.

4   Stir in the sesame oil, kecap manis and chilli
sauce and toss to heat through. Scatter with the
sesame seeds and serve immediately.

NUTRITION PER SERVE
Protein 18.5 g; Fat 20 g; Carbohydrate 7 g; Dietary
Fibre 7 g; Cholesterol 0 mg; 1232 kJ (293 Cal)

Put the tofu in a bowl with the ginger and soy
sauce and leave to marinate.

Add the marinated tofu and the garlic and stir-fry
for 3 minutes, or until golden.

Thai noodles with bean curd

PREPARATION TIME: 25 MINUTES + 20 MINUTES SOAKING | TOTAL COOKING TIME: 5–7 MINUTES | SERVES 4–6

8 dried Chinese mushrooms
250 g (9 oz) rice vermicelli
2 tablespoons oil
3 garlic cloves, chopped
5 cm (2 inch) piece fresh ginger, grated
100 g (3½ oz) deep-fried tofu puffs, cut into
　　small pieces
1 carrot, cut into matchsticks
100 g (3½ oz) green beans, cut into
　　short lengths
½ red capsicum (pepper), cut into
　　matchsticks
2 tablespoons soy sauce
1 tablespoon fish sauce
2 teaspoons soft brown sugar
100 g (3½ oz) bean sprouts
90 g (3¼ oz/1¼ cup) finely shredded cabbage
60 g (2¼ oz/⅔ cup) bean sprouts, extra,
　　straggly ends removed, to garnish
chilli sauce, for serving

1　Soak the dried Chinese mushrooms in hot water for 20 minutes. Drain and then slice.

2　In a heatproof bowl, pour boiling water over the vermicelli and soak for 1–4 minutes, or until soft. Drain.

3　Heat a wok, add the oil and swirl to coat the sides. When very hot, add the garlic, ginger and tofu and stir-fry for 1 minute. Add the carrot, beans, capsicum and mushrooms to the wok and stir-fry for 2 minutes. Add the sauces and sugar and toss well. Cover the wok and steam for 1 minute.

4　Add the vermicelli, bean sprouts and all but a few tablespoonfuls of cabbage. Toss, cover and steam for 30 seconds. Arrange the noodles on a serving plate and garnish with the extra bean sprouts and remaining cabbage and serve with chilli sauce.

NUTRITION PER SERVE (6)
Protein 5 g; Fat 8.5 g; Carbohydrate 15 g; Dietary
Fibre 5 g; Cholesterol 0 mg; 656 kJ (157 Cal)

Cut the deep-fried tofu puffs into small cubes, using a sharp knife.

Place the vermicelli noodles into a heatproof bowl and pour boiling water over them.

Stir-fry the garlic, ginger and tofu in the hot oil for 1 minute.

Vegetables

Potato noodles with vegetables

PREPARATION TIME: 30 MINUTES + SOAKING | TOTAL COOKING TIME: 25 MINUTES | SERVES 4

300 g (10½ oz) dried potato starch noodles

30 g (1 oz) dried black fungus

60 ml (2 fl oz/¼ cup) sesame oil

2 tablespoons vegetable oil

3 garlic cloves, finely chopped

4 cm (1½ inch) piece fresh ginger, grated

2 spring onions (scallions), finely chopped

2 carrots, cut into short matchsticks

2 spring onions (scallions), extra, cut into
     short lengths

500 g (1 lb 2 oz) baby bok choy or 250 g
     (9 oz) English spinach, roughly chopped

60 ml (2 fl oz/¼ cup) Japanese soy sauce

2 tablespoons mirin

1 teaspoon sugar

2 tablespoons sesame seed and
     seaweed sprinkle (see NOTE)

NUTRITION PER SERVE
Protein 5 g; Fat 11 g; Carbohydrate 20 g; Dietary
Fibre 3 g; Cholesterol 0 mg; 830 kJ (198 Cal)

1 Cook the dried potato noodles in boiling water for about 5 minutes, or until translucent. Drain and then rinse under cold running water until cold. (Thoroughly rinsing the noodles will remove any excess starch.) Roughly chop the noodles into lengths of about 15 cm (6 inches), to make them easier to eat with chopsticks.

2 Pour boiling water over the fungus and soak for 10 minutes. Drain thoroughly and chop roughly. Heat 1 tablespoon of the sesame oil with the vegetable oil in a large, heavy-based pan or wok. Add the garlic, ginger and spring onion to the pan and cook for 3 minutes over medium heat, stirring regularly. Add the carrot sticks and stir-fry for 1 minute.

3 Add the noodles, extra spring onion, bok choy, remaining sesame oil, soy sauce, mirin and sugar. Toss well, cover and cook over low heat for 2 minutes.

4 Add the drained fungus, cover the pan and cook for another 2 minutes. Sprinkle with the sesame seed and seaweed sprinkle. Serve immediately.

NOTE: *A Japanese seasoning normally sprinkled over rice or noodles.*

Make the noodles easier to eat by roughly chopping them with scissors.

Add the noodles, spring onion, bok choy, sesame oil, soy sauce, mirin and sugar.

Green beans with shiitake mushrooms

PREPARATION TIME: 15 MINUTES | TOTAL COOKING TIME: 12 MINUTES | SERVES 4

2 tablespoons sesame seeds
1 tablespoon oil
1 teaspoon sesame oil
5 spring onions (scallions), sliced, plus extra
    finely shredded spring onion, to garnish
800 g (1 lb 12 oz) green beans
200 g (7 oz) shiitake mushrooms
2 teaspoons finely chopped fresh ginger
2 tablespoons mirin
2 tablespoons soy sauce
1 tablespoon sugar

1   Heat the wok until very hot, add the sesame seeds and dry-fry over high heat until they are golden. Remove from the wok and set aside.

2   Reheat the wok, add the oils and swirl to coat the side. Add the spring onion and beans, and stir-fry for 4 minutes. Add the mushrooms and ginger, and cook for 4 minutes.

3   Pour in the mirin, soy sauce and sugar, cover and cook for 2 minutes, or until the beans are tender. Sprinkle with the toasted sesame seeds and serve immediately, garnished with the shredded spring onion.

NUTRITION PER SERVE
Protein 7.5 g; Fat 12 g; Carbohydrate 10 g; Dietary Fibre 7 g; Cholesterol 0 mg; 885 kJ (210 Cal)

Peel the fresh ginger and chop it finely to make up 2 teaspoons.

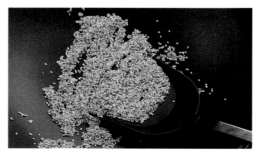

Dry-fry the sesame seeds over high heat until they are golden.

Stir-fry the spring onion and beans in the oil and sesame oil.

Mushrooms with Thai basil

PREPARATION TIME: 10 MINUTES | TOTAL COOKING TIME: 6 MINUTES | SERVES 4

1 tablespoon oil

2.5 cm (1 inch) piece fresh galangal, finely sliced

2 garlic cloves, crushed

2 red chillies, finely chopped

200 g (7 oz) button mushrooms, halved

100 g (3½ oz) oyster mushrooms, halved

1 tablespoon fish sauce

1 teaspoon soy sauce

1 very large handful Thai basil, roughly chopped

1 Heat the oil in a wok and stir-fry the galangal, garlic and chilli for 2 minutes. Add the button mushrooms and stir-fry for 2 minutes. Add the oyster mushrooms and stir-fry for 30 seconds, until softened.

2 Add the fish sauce, soy sauce and chopped basil and toss well. Serve immediately.

VARIATION: *You can use fresh shiitake, Swiss brown, straw or any other variety of fresh mushroom.*

NUTRITION PER SERVE
Protein 3 g; Fat 5 g; Carbohydrate 2 g; Dietary Fibre 2 g; Cholesterol 0 mg; 275 kJ (65 Cal)

Fresh galangal is similar to fresh ginger. Peel it and then finely slice it.

Cook the oyster mushrooms briefly, until they begin to soften.

Toss in the fish sauce, soy sauce and chopped basil.

Thai-spiced cauliflower and snake beans

PREPARATION TIME: 10 MINUTES | TOTAL COOKING TIME: 10 MINUTES | SERVES 4

4 coriander (cilantro) roots or 1 tablespoon
    chopped leaves and stems
1 teaspoon soft brown sugar
½ teaspoon ground turmeric
2 garlic cloves, crushed
2 tablespoons fish sauce
2 tablespoons oil
4 garlic cloves, extra, sliced
20 English spinach leaves, shredded
400 g (14 oz) cauliflower, cut into florets
200 g (7 oz) snake beans, cut into
    short lengths
6 spring onions (scallions), cut into
    short lengths
1 tablespoon lime juice

NUTRITION PER SERVE
Protein 6.9 g; Fat 10 g; Carbohydrate 6.7 g; Dietary
Fibre 6.8 g; Cholesterol 0 mg; 657 kJ (157 Cal)

1 Using a mortar and pestle or a blender, blend the coriander, sugar, turmeric, crushed garlic and 1 tablespoon of the fish sauce to make a smooth paste.

2 Heat half the oil in a wok, add the sliced garlic and stir-fry for 30 seconds, or until just beginning to brown. Do not allow it to burn or it will be bitter.

3 Add the spinach to the wok and stir-fry for 30 seconds, or until just wilted. Add ½ teaspoon cracked black pepper and the remaining fish sauce and mix well. Arrange on a serving plate and keep warm.

4 Heat the remaining oil in the wok, add the paste and cook over high heat for 1 minute, or until aromatic. Add the cauliflower and stir-fry until well combined. Add 125 ml (4 fl oz/½ cup) water and bring to the boil. Reduce the heat and simmer, covered, for 3 minutes. Add the beans, cover and cook for another 3 minutes. Add the spring onions and stir until just wilted. Spoon the vegetables over the spinach and drizzle with lime juice to serve.

Wash the snake beans, hold them in bunches and cut them into short lengths.

Add the extra sliced garlic to the hot oil and stir-fry briefly until it starts to brown.

Stir in the remaining fish sauce and the pepper and then toss to combine.

Red vegetable curry

PREPARATION TIME: 25 MINUTES I TOTAL COOKING TIME: 30 MINUTES I SERVES 4

1 tablespoon oil

1 onion, chopped

1–2 tablespoons red curry paste, to taste

375 ml (13 fl oz/1½ cups) coconut milk

2 potatoes, peeled and chopped

200 g (7 oz) cauliflower florets

6 makrut (kaffir lime) leaves (see NOTE, page 33)

150 g (5½ oz) snake beans, cut into short lengths

½ red capsicum (pepper), sliced

10 fresh baby corn spears, cut in half lengthways (see HINT)

1 tablespoon green peppercorns, roughly chopped

1 small handful Thai basil leaves, finely chopped

2 tablespoons fish sauce

1 tablespoon lime juice

2 teaspoons soft brown sugar

1   Heat the oil in a large wok and stir-fry the onion and curry paste for 4 minutes over medium heat.

2   Add the coconut milk and 250 ml (9 fl oz/ 1 cup) water, bring to the boil and simmer for 5 minutes. Add the potatoes, cauliflower and makrut leaves and simmer for 7 minutes. Add the snake beans, capsicum, corn and peppercorns and cook for 5 minutes, or until the vegetables are tender.

3   Add the basil, fish sauce, lime juice and sugar just before serving.

HINT: *You could use tinned corn spears—add just before serving.*

Stir the chopped onion and curry paste in a wok for 4 minutes over medium heat.

Add the snake beans, capsicum, corn and peppercorns and cook until tender.

NUTRITION PER SERVE
Protein 7.5 g; Fat 24 g; Carbohydrate 23 g; Dietary Fibre 6 g; Cholesterol 0 mg; 1414 kJ (338 Cal)

Vegetables stir-fried in coconut milk

PREPARATION TIME: 20 MINUTES | TOTAL COOKING TIME: 15 MINUTES | SERVES 4

2 tablespoons oil
2 garlic cloves, chopped
5 cm (2 inch) piece fresh ginger, grated
2 teaspoons green peppercorns
1 eggplant (aubergine), diced
1 small sweet potato, diced
100 g (3½ oz) green beans, cut into
    short lengths
200 g (7 oz) asparagus, cut into short lengths
125 ml (4 fl oz/½ cup) coconut milk
2 teaspoons fish sauce
12 English spinach leaves, trimmed
1 medium handful Thai basil leaves

1   Heat the oil in a wok. Add the garlic, ginger and peppercorns and stir-fry for 30 seconds. Add the eggplant, sweet potato and 2 teaspoons water and stir-fry over medium heat for 5 minutes.

2   Add the beans to the wok, cover and steam for 4 minutes, shaking the wok occasionally to prevent the vegetables from sticking.

3   Add the asparagus and coconut milk to the wok and stir-fry for 3 minutes, or until the asparagus is just tender. Add the fish sauce, spinach and basil and toss until softened slightly. Serve immediately.

VARIATION: *Use broccoli or cabbage instead of spinach. Cook a little longer.*

Add the diced eggplant, sweet potato and water to the wok. Cook for 5 minutes.

Cover the wok after adding the beans and steam the vegetables for 4 minutes.

NUTRITION PER SERVE
Protein 3.5 g; Fat 16 g; Carbohydrate 10 g; Dietary Fibre 4 g; Cholesterol 0 mg; 826 kJ (197 Cal)

Asian greens and mushrooms

PREPARATION TIME: 20 MINUTES | TOTAL COOKING TIME: 5 MINUTES | SERVES 4

20 Chinese broccoli stems

4 baby bok choy

100 g (3½ oz) shimeji or enoki mushrooms

100 g (3½ oz) shiitake mushrooms

1 tablespoon soy sauce

2 teaspoons crushed palm sugar (jaggery)

1 tablespoon oil

4 spring onions (scallions), cut into
    short pieces

5 cm (2 inch) piece fresh ginger, cut into
    thin strips

1–2 small red chillies, seeded and
    finely chopped

2–3 garlic cloves, crushed

125 g (4½ oz) snow peas (mangetouts),
    halved

1–2 teaspoons seasoning sauce

1 Remove any tough outer leaves from the Chinese broccoli and bok choy. Cut into 4 cm (1½ inch) pieces across the leaves, including the stems. Wash thoroughly, then drain and dry thoroughly. Wipe the mushrooms with a paper towel and trim the ends. Slice the shiitake mushrooms thickly.

2 Combine the soy sauce and palm sugar with 60 ml (2 fl oz/¼ cup) water. Set aside.

3 Heat the wok until very hot, add the oil and swirl it around to coat the side. Stir-fry the spring onion, ginger, chilli and garlic over low heat for 30 seconds, without browning. Increase the heat to high and add the Chinese broccoli, bok choy and snow peas. Stir-fry for 1–2 minutes, or until the vegetables are wilted.

4 Add the prepared mushrooms and soy sauce mixture. Stir-fry over high heat for 1–2 minutes, or until the mushrooms and sauce are heated through. Sprinkle with the seasoning sauce, to taste, and serve immediately.

NUTRITION PER SERVE
Protein 6.5 g; Fat 10 g; Carbohydrate 15 g; Dietary Fibre 3 g; Cholesterol 0 mg; 780 kJ (185 Cal)

You will need to gently separate the shimeji mushrooms from each other.

Trim the shiitake mushrooms and cut them into thick slices.

Peel the piece of ginger and cut it into thin strips with a very sharp knife.

Fragrant greens

PREPARATION TIME: 15 MINUTES | TOTAL COOKING TIME: 8 MINUTES | SERVES 4

2 tablespoons oil
300 g (10½ oz) broccoli, cut into small florets
150 g (5½ oz) snake beans, cut into
    short lengths
3 spring onions (scallions), sliced
250 g (9 oz) cabbage, finely shredded
1 green capsicum (pepper), sliced
2 tablespoons lime juice
1 tablespoon soft brown sugar
1 medium handful Thai basil, shredded, plus
    extra leaves, to garnish (see HINT)

1 Heat the wok until very hot, add the oil and swirl it around to coat the side. Stir-fry the broccoli and snake beans for 3–4 minutes, or until the vegetables are bright green and just tender. Add the spring onion, cabbage and capsicum, and continue stir-frying until just softened.

2 Combine the lime juice and brown sugar, stirring until the sugar has dissolved. Add to the wok with the basil. Toss to combine with the vegetables and serve immediately, garnished with the extra basil leaves.

HINT: *You can include any suitable kind of green vegetable in this dish, including Asian greens. If you can't find Thai basil, use ordinary basil or coriander—either will give fragrance and flavour like Thai basil.*

Top and tail the snake beans and cut them into short lengths.

Using a large sharp knife, finely shred the cabbage so that it will stir-fry quickly.

NUTRITION PER SERVE
Protein 6 g; Fat 10 g; Carbohydrate 9 g; Dietary Fibre 7 g; Cholesterol 0 mg; 630 kJ (150 Cal)

Tamari almonds with spicy green beans

PREPARATION TIME: 10 MINUTES | TOTAL COOKING TIME: 25 MINUTES | SERVES 4–6

1 tablespoon sesame oil

500 g (1 lb 2 oz/2½ cups) jasmine rice

2 tablespoons sesame oil, extra

1 long red chilli, seeded and finely chopped

2 cm (¾ inch) piece of fresh ginger, peeled
   and grated

2 garlic cloves, crushed

375 g (13 oz) green beans, chopped

125 ml (4 fl oz/½ cup) hoisin sauce

1 tablespoon soft brown sugar

2 tablespoons mirin

250 g (9 oz) tamari roasted almonds, roughly
   chopped (see HINT)

1 Preheat the oven to moderately hot
200°C (400°F/Gas 6). Heat the oil in a 1.5 litre
(52 fl oz/6 cup) ovenproof dish. Add the rice
and stir to coat with the oil. Stir in 1 litre
(35 fl oz/4 cups) boiling water. Cover and bake
for 20 minutes, or until all the water has been
absorbed. Keep warm.

2 Meanwhile, heat the extra oil in a wok or
large frying pan and cook the chilli, ginger and
garlic for 1 minute, or until lightly browned.
Add the beans, hoisin sauce and sugar and
stir-fry for 2 minutes. Stir in the mirin and
cook for 1 minute, or until the beans are tender
but still crunchy.

3 Remove from the heat and stir in the
almonds. Serve on a bed of the rice.

HINT: *Tamari roasted almonds are available from
health-food stores.*

NUTRITION PER SERVE (6)
Protein 15 g; Fat 34 g; Carbohydrate 80 g; Dietary
Fibre 9.5 g; Cholesterol 0 mg; 2874 kJ (687 Cal)

When chopping chillies, it's a good idea to wear
disposable rubber gloves to prevent chilli burns.

Cook the rice in the oven until all the water has
been absorbed.

Curried sweet potato

PREPARATION TIME: 25 MINUTES | TOTAL COOKING TIME: 30 MINUTES | SERVES 4–6

1 tablespoon oil

1 onion, chopped

1–2 tablespoons green curry paste, to taste

375 ml (13 fl oz/1½ cups) coconut milk

300 g (10½ oz) sweet potato, peeled
    and cubed

1 eggplant (aubergine), quartered and sliced

6 makrut (kaffir lime) leaves (see NOTE,
    page 33)

2 tablespoons fish sauce

2 tablespoons lime juice

2 teaspoons lime zest

2 teaspoons soft brown sugar

coriander (cilantro) leaves

NUTRITION PER SERVE (6)
Protein 3 g; Fat 16 g; Carbohydrate 14 g; Dietary
Fibre 3 g; Cholesterol 0 mg; 862 kJ (205 Cal)

1   Heat the oil in a large wok and stir-fry the onion and curry paste for 3 minutes over medium heat.

2   Add the coconut milk and 250 ml (9 fl oz/ 1 cup) water to the wok. Bring to the boil then reduce the heat and simmer for 5 minutes. Add the sweet potato and cook for 6 minutes.

3   Add the eggplant and makrut leaves to the wok and cook for 10 minutes, or until the vegetables are very tender, stirring often.

4   Add the fish sauce, lime juice and zest, and sugar and toss. Sprinkle with fresh coriander leaves to serve.

HINT: *Traditional Thai, pea eggplants can be used instead of the sliced eggplant. Add them to the curry about 6 minutes before serving. The pea eggplants are available, when in season, from Asian fruit and vegetable speciality stores.*

Peel the sweet potato and cut into even-sized cubes for quick cooking.

When simmering the coconut milk, don't cover the wok or the milk will curdle.

Add the eggplant and makrut leaves to the wok and cook until tender.

Chilli noodles and nuts

PREPARATION TIME: 20 MINUTES | TOTAL COOKING TIME: 12 MINUTES | SERVES 4

1½ tablespoons oil
1 tablespoon sesame oil
2–3 small red chillies, finely chopped
1 large onion, cut into thin wedges
4 garlic cloves, very thinly sliced
1 red capsicum (pepper), cut into strips, plus
    extra finely sliced, to garnish
1 green capsicum (pepper), cut into strips
2 large carrots, cut into batons
100 g (3½ oz) green beans
2 celery stalks, cut into batons
2 teaspoons honey
500 g (1 lb 2 oz) hokkien (egg) noodles,
    gently separated
100 g (3½ oz) dry-roasted peanuts
100 g (3½ oz/⅔ cup) honey-roasted cashews
30 g (1 oz) snipped garlic chives, or 4 spring
    onions (scallions), chopped
sweet chilli sauce and sesame oil, to serve

1 Heat the wok over low heat, add the oils and swirl them to coat the side. When the oil is warm, add the chilli and heat until the oil is very hot.

2 Add the onion and garlic and stir-fry for 1 minute, or until the onion just softens. Add the capsicum, carrot and beans and stir-fry for 1 minute. Add the celery, honey and 1 tablespoon water, and season with salt and pepper. Toss well, then cover and cook for 1–2 minutes, or until the vegetables are just tender.

3 Add the noodles and nuts and toss well. Cook, covered, for 1–2 minutes, or until the noodles are heated through. Stir in the garlic chives and serve, drizzled with the sweet chilli sauce and sesame oil. Garnish with the finely sliced capsicum.

Peel the cloves of garlic, then cut them into paper-thin slices.

Remove the seeds from the capsicum and cut the flesh into strips.

NUTRITION PER SERVE
Protein 20 g; Fat 45 g; Carbohydrate 75 g; Dietary Fibre 7 g; Cholesterol 0 mg; 3330 kJ (795 Cal)

Eggplant with hot bean sauce

PREPARATION TIME: 20 MINUTES | TOTAL COOKING TIME: 15 MINUTES | SERVES 4–6

60 ml (2 fl oz/¼ cup) peanut oil
800 g (1 lb 12 oz) eggplant (aubergine), cut
   into small cubes
4 spring onions (scallions), chopped
3 garlic cloves, crushed
1 tablespoon finely chopped fresh ginger
1 tablespoon hot bean paste
125 ml (4 fl oz/½ cup) vegetable stock
60 ml (2 fl oz/¼ cup) Chinese rice wine
2 tablespoons rice vinegar
1 tablespoon tomato paste
   (concentrated purée)
2 teaspoons soft brown sugar
2 tablespoons soy sauce
1 teaspoon cornflour (cornstarch)
2 tablespoons basil leaves, to serve

1   Heat a wok until very hot, add 1 tablespoon peanut oil and swirl to coat. Stir-fry the eggplant in batches for 3–4 minutes, or until browned. Remove from the wok.

2   Reheat the wok, add the remaining oil and stir-fry the spring onion, garlic, ginger and bean paste for 30 seconds. Add the stock, rice wine, rice vinegar, tomato paste, sugar and soy and stir-fry for 1 minute.

3   Mix the cornflour with 1 tablespoon water, add to the wok and bring to the boil. Return the eggplant to the wok and stir-fry for 2–3 minutes to cook through. Sprinkle with basil to serve.

NUTRITION PER SERVE (6)
Protein 2 g; Fat 10 g; Carbohydrate 5.5 g; Dietary
Fibre 3.5 g; Cholesterol 0 mg; 550 kJ (130 Cal)

You don't need to peel the eggplant before cooking it. Simply cut it into cubes.

Stir-fry the spring onion, garlic, ginger and bean paste for 30 seconds.

Asparagus stir-fried with mustard

PREPARATION TIME: 10 MINUTES | TOTAL COOKING TIME: 10 MINUTES | SERVES 2

480 g (1 lb 1 oz) asparagus
1 tablespoon oil
1 red onion, sliced
1 garlic clove, crushed
1 tablespoon wholegrain mustard
1 teaspoon honey
125 ml (4 fl oz/½ cup) pouring
    (whipping) cream

1 Break the woody ends off the asparagus by holding both ends of the spear and bending gently until it snaps at its natural breaking point. Cut the asparagus into 5 cm (2 inch) lengths.

2 Heat the wok until very hot, add the oil and swirl to coat the side. Stir-fry the onion for 2–3 minutes, or until tender. Stir in the crushed garlic and cook for 1 minute. Add the asparagus to the wok and stir-fry for 3–4 minutes, or until tender, being careful not to overcook the asparagus.

3 Remove the asparagus from the wok, set it aside and keep it warm. Combine the wholegrain mustard, honey and cream. Add to the wok and bring to the boil, then reduce the heat and simmer for 2–3 minutes, or until the mixture reduces and thickens slightly. Return the asparagus to the wok and toss it through the cream mixture. Serve immediately.

VARIATION: *When asparagus is in season, white and purple asparagus are also available. Vary the recipe by using a mixture of the three colours. Do not overcook the purple asparagus or it will turn green as it cooks.*

HINT: *This dish can also be served on croutons, toasted ciabatta or toasted wholegrain bread as a smart starter or first course.*

NUTRITION PER SERVE
Protein 8.5 g; Fat 35 g; Carbohydrate 10 g; Dietary Fibre 5 g; Cholesterol 85 mg; 1685 kJ (405 Cal)

Gently bend the asparagus spear and the tough woody end will naturally snap off.

Stir-fry the sliced red onion over moderate heat for 2–3 minutes, or until tender.

Udon noodles with vegetables

PREPARATION TIME: 15 MINUTES I TOTAL COOKING TIME: 10 MINUTES I SERVES 4

500 g (1 lb 2 oz) fresh udon noodles
1 tablespoon oil
6 spring onions (scallions), cut into
    short lengths
3 garlic cloves, crushed
1 tablespoon grated fresh ginger
2 carrots, cut into short lengths
150 g (5½ oz) snow peas (mangetouts), cut in
    half on the diagonal
100 g (3½ oz) bean sprouts
500 g (1 lb 2 oz) choy sum, cut into
    short lengths
2 tablespoons Japanese soy sauce
2 tablespoons mirin
2 tablespoons kecap manis (see NOTE,
    page 18)
2 sheets roasted nori, cut into thin strips,
    extra, to garnish

1   Bring a saucepan of water to the boil, add the noodles and cook for 5 minutes, or until tender and not clumped together. Drain and rinse under hot water.

2   Heat the oil in a wok until hot, then add the spring onion, garlic and ginger. Stir-fry over high heat for 1–2 minutes, or until soft. Add the carrot, snow peas and 1 tablespoon water, toss well, cover and cook for 1–2 minutes, or until the vegetables are just tender.

3   Add the noodles, bean sprouts, choy sum, soy sauce, mirin and kecap manis, then toss until the choy sum is wilted and coated with the sauce. Stir in the nori just before serving. Garnish with the extra nori.

Cut the roasted nori sheets into very thin strips. It is available from Asian speciality shops.

Cook the udon noodles until they are tender and not clumped together.

NUTRITION PER SERVE
Protein 25 g; Fat 7.5 g; Carbohydrate 95 g; Dietary Fibre 13 g; Cholesterol 0 mg; 2330 kJ (557 Cal)

Vegetables with honey and soy

PREPARATION TIME: 15 MINUTES | TOTAL COOKING TIME: 5 MINUTES | SERVES 4

1 tablespoon sesame seeds
1 tablespoon oil
1 teaspoon sesame oil
1 garlic clove, crushed
2 teaspoons grated fresh ginger
2 spring onions (scallions), thinly sliced
250 g (9 oz) broccoli, cut into small florets
1 red capsicum (pepper), thinly sliced
1 green capsicum (pepper), thinly sliced
150 g (5½ oz) button mushrooms, halved
30 g (1 oz/¼ cup) halved pitted black olives
1 tablespoon soy sauce
1 tablespoon honey
1 tablespoon sweet chilli sauce

1   Place the sesame seeds on an oven tray and toast under a hot grill (broiler) for a couple of minutes, or until they are golden. Heat a wok, add the oils and swirl to coat the base and side of the wok. Add the garlic, ginger and spring onion and stir-fry for 1 minute.

2   Add the broccoli, capsicum, mushrooms and olives to the wok. Stir-fry for a further 2 minutes, or until the vegetables are just tender.

3   Combine the soy sauce, honey and chilli sauce in a bowl. Pour over the vegetables and then toss lightly. Sprinkle with the toasted sesame seeds and serve immediately.

Stir-fry the vegetables until they are just tender but keep their bright colours.

NUTRITION PER SERVE
Protein 6 g; Fat 8 g; Carbohydrate 9 g; Dietary
Fibre 5 g; Cholesterol 0 mg; 550 kJ (130 Cal)

Sweet and sour noodles

PREPARATION TIME: 12 MINUTES | TOTAL COOKING TIME: 15 MINUTES | SERVES 4–6

200 g (7 oz) thin fresh egg noodles
3 tablespoons oil
1 green capsicum (pepper), sliced
1 red capsicum (pepper), sliced
2 celery stalks, sliced diagonally
1 carrot, sliced diagonally
250 g (9 oz) button mushrooms, sliced
4 fresh baby corn spears, sliced diagonally
3 teaspoons cornflour (cornstarch)
2 tablespoons brown vinegar
1 teaspoon chopped fresh chilli
2 teaspoons tomato paste
    (concentrated purée)
2 chicken stock (bouillon) cubes, crumbled
1 teaspoon sesame oil
450 g (1 lb) tin chopped pineapple pieces
3 spring onions (scallions), sliced diagonally,
    plus extra finely shredded spring onion,
    to garnish

1 Cook the noodles in boiling water for 3 minutes; drain well. Heat the oil in a wok and stir-fry the capsicum, celery, carrot and mushrooms over high heat for 5 minutes.

2 Add the corn and noodles to the wok. Reduce the heat to low and cook for 2 minutes.

3 Blend the cornflour and vinegar into a smooth paste. Add the chilli, tomato paste, stock cubes, oil and undrained pineapple to the paste and stir well.

4 Pour the pineapple mixture into the wok. Stir over medium heat for 5 minutes, or until the sauce has boiled and thickened. Stir in the spring onions and serve immediately. Garnish with the shredded spring onion.

VARIATION: *Thinly sliced Chinese barbecued pork (char siu) can be added to this stir-fry.*

NUTRITION PER SERVE (6)
Protein 8 g; Fat 12 g; Carbohydrate 36 g; Dietary Fibre 5 g; Cholesterol 6 mg; 1182 kJ (282 Cal)

Slice the celery, carrot and baby corn on the diagonal for an attractive stir-fry.

Cook the capsicum, celery, carrot and mushrooms, before adding the corn and noodles.

Stir in the spring onions just before serving, once the sauce has thickened.

Thai wok-curried vegetables

PREPARATION TIME: 25 MINUTES | TOTAL COOKING TIME: 20 MINUTES | SERVES 4–6

1 tablespoon oil

1 onion, finely chopped

1–2 tablespoons green curry paste

375 ml (13 fl oz/1½ cups) coconut milk

100 g (3½ oz) snake beans, cut into
    short lengths

1 red capsicum (pepper), sliced

150 g (5½ oz) broccoli, cut into florets

4 makrut (kaffir lime) leaves (see NOTE,
    page 33)

2 zucchini (courgettes), sliced

150 g (5½ oz/2 cups) shredded cabbage

2 tablespoons fish sauce

2 tablespoons lime juice

2 teaspoons finely grated lime zest

2 teaspoons soft brown sugar

1   Heat the oil in a large wok. Add the onion
and curry paste and stir-fry for 3 minutes over
medium heat. Add the coconut milk and
250 ml (9 fl oz/1 cup) water and bring to the
boil, stirring. Reduce the heat and simmer for
5 minutes.

2   Add the snake beans, capsicum, broccoli and
makrut leaves and simmer for 5 minutes. Add the
zucchini and cabbage and simmer for 3 minutes,
or until softened.

3   Add the fish sauce, lime juice and zest and
brown sugar and toss together before serving.

VARIATION: *A Thai green curry can be made
with just about any mix of vegetables. Celery or
green beans could be used instead of snake beans.*

Wash the snake beans, hold them in bunches and
cut them into short lengths.

Add the sliced zucchini and the shredded cabbage
to the wok. Cook for 3 minutes.

NUTRITION PER SERVE (6)
Protein 4.5 g; Fat 14 g; Carbohydrate 6.5 g; Dietary
Fibre 4.5 g; Cholesterol 0 mg; 712 kJ (170 Cal)

Mushroom noodles

PREPARATION TIME: 30 MINUTES + 20 MINUTES SOAKING | TOTAL COOKING TIME: 15 MINUTES | SERVES 4–6

30 g (1 oz) dried Chinese mushrooms
1 tablespoon oil
½ teaspoon sesame oil
1 tablespoon grated fresh ginger
4 garlic cloves, crushed
100 g (3½ oz) shiitake mushrooms,
   trimmed, sliced
150 g (5½ oz) oyster mushrooms, sliced
150 g (5½ oz) shimeji mushrooms, trimmed,
   pulled apart
185 ml (6 fl oz/¾ cup) dashi granules
60 ml (2 fl oz/¼ cup) soy sauce
60 ml (2 fl oz/¼ cup) mirin
30 g (1 oz) butter
2 tablespoons lemon juice
100 g (3½ oz) enoki mushrooms, trimmed,
   pulled apart
500 g (1 lb 2 oz) thin hokkien (egg) noodles,
   separated
1 tablespoon snipped chives

1   Soak the Chinese mushrooms in 375 ml
(13 fl oz/1½ cups) boiling water for 20 minutes,
or until soft. Drain, reserving the liquid. Discard
the stems and slice the caps. Heat a wok until
very hot, add the oils and swirl to coat. Add
the ginger, garlic, shiitake, oyster and shimeji
mushrooms and stir-fry for 2 minutes, or until
wilted. Remove from the wok.

2   Combine the dashi, soy sauce, mirin,
¼ teaspoon white pepper and 185 ml (6 fl oz/
¾ cup) reserved liquid, add to the wok and cook
for 3 minutes. Add the butter, lemon juice and
1 teaspoon salt and cook for 1 minute, or until
the sauce thickens. Return the mushrooms to
the wok, cook for 2 minutes, then stir in the
enoki and Chinese mushrooms. Add the noodles
and stir for 3 minutes, or until heated through.
Sprinkle with chives to serve.

NUTRITION PER SERVE (6)
Protein 15 g; Fat 8.5 g; Carbohydrate 60 g; Dietary
Fibre 5 g; Cholesterol 25 mg; 1610 kJ (385 Cal)

Soak the Chinese mushrooms in boiling water,
then drain, reserving the liquid.

Stir-fry the mushrooms for 1–2 minutes, or until
they have wilted.

Basics—curry
pastes and more

Curry pastes

Green curry paste

MAKES APPROXIMATELY 1 CUP

Dry-fry 1 tablespoon coriander seeds and 2 teaspoons cumin seeds in a wok for 2–3 minutes, allow to cool, then finely grind in a mortar and pestle or spice grinder with 1 teaspoon black peppercorns. Wrap 2 teaspoons shrimp paste in foil and cook under a hot grill (broiler) for 3 minutes, turning twice. Process the ground spices and shrimp paste for 5 seconds. Add the following ingredients: 8 roughly chopped, large fresh green chillies, 4 chopped French shallots (eschalots), 5 cm (2 inch) pounded or chopped piece fresh galangal, 12 chopped, small garlic cloves, 60 g (2 oz) chopped coriander (cilantro) leaves, stems and roots, 6 chopped makrut (kaffir lime) leaves, 3 finely chopped lemongrass stems (white part only), 2 teaspoons grated lime zest, 2 teaspoons salt and 2 tablespoons oil. Process for 20 seconds at a time, scraping down the sides of the bowl with a spatula from time to time, until the mixture forms a smooth paste.

Musaman curry paste

MAKES APPROXIMATELY 1 CUP

Dry-fry 1 tablespoon coriander seeds, 1 tablespoon cumin seeds and the seeds from 4 cardamom pods in a wok for 2–3 minutes. Place the spices and 2 teaspoons black peppercorns in a mortar and pestle or spice grinder and finely grind. Place the ground spices and the following ingredients in a food processor: 1 tablespoon shrimp paste, 1 teaspoon grated nutmeg, ½ teaspoon ground cloves, 15 dried red chillies, 3 chopped French shallots (eschalots), 2 finely chopped lemongrass stems (white part only), 6 chopped small garlic cloves and 1 tablespoon oil. Process for 20 seconds and scrape down the side of the bowl with a spatula. Continue processing for 5 seconds at a time until the mixture forms a smooth paste.

Panang curry paste

MAKES APPROXIMATELY 1 CUP

Trim the stems from 8 large dried red chillies and soak them in 125 ml (4 fl oz/½ cup) hot water for 30 minutes. Wrap 2 teaspoons of shrimp paste in foil and cook under a hot grill (broiler) for 2–3 minutes, turning the package twice. Place the softened chillies and soaking water, shrimp paste, 3 chopped French shallots (eschalots), 5 cm (2 inch) pounded or chopped piece fresh galangal, 12 chopped small garlic cloves, 4 chopped coriander (cilantro) roots, 3 finely chopped lemongrass stems (white part only), 1 tablespoon grated lime zest, 1 teaspoon black peppercorns and 2 tablespoons oil in a food processor. Process for 20 seconds at a time, scraping down the side of the bowl with a spatula each time, until the mixture forms a smooth paste. Add 1 tablespoon of fish sauce, 1 teaspoon salt and 125 g (4 oz/½ cup) crunchy peanut butter; process for 10 seconds, or until combined.

Red curry paste

MAKES APPROXIMATELY 1 CUP

Dry-fry 1 tablespoon coriander seeds and 2 teaspoons cumin seeds in a wok for 2–3 minutes, then finely grind in a mortar and pestle or spice grinder with 1 teaspoon of black peppercorns. Wrap 2 teaspoons shrimp paste in foil and cook under a hot grill (broiler) for 3 minutes, turning twice. Process the ground spices, roasted shrimp paste, 1 teaspoon ground nutmeg and 12 roughly chopped, dried or fresh red chillies for 5 seconds. Add the following ingredients and process for 20 seconds at a time until you have a smooth paste: 4 chopped French shallots (eschalots), 2 tablespoons of oil, 4 finely chopped lemongrass stems (white part only), 12 small chopped garlic cloves, 2 tablespoons chopped coriander (cilantro) roots, 2 tablespoons chopped coriander (cilantro) stems, 6 chopped makrut (kaffir lime) leaves, 2 teaspoons grated lime zest, 2 teaspoons salt, 2 teaspoons ground turmeric and 1 teaspoon paprika.

Serving sauces

Basic sauce (nam prik)

MAKES APPROXIMATELY 125 ML (4 FL OZ/½ CUP)

In a bowl, combine 3 tablespoons fish sauce, 1 tablespoon white vinegar, 2–3 teaspoons finely chopped fresh red chillies, 1 teaspoon sugar and 2 teaspoons chopped fresh coriander (cilantro) stems and stir until the sugar dissolves.

Cooked hot chilli sauce

MAKES APPROXIMATELY 125 ML (4 FL OZ/½ CUP)

Chop 2 garlic cloves and combine in a dry frying pan with 2 finely chopped lemongrass stems, 6 chopped French shallots (eschalots), 2–4 tablespoons chopped, fresh red chillies and 2 chopped coriander (cilantro) roots. Stir for 5 minutes over low heat and then allow to cool. Place in a food processor with 2 teaspoons shrimp paste and 2 tablespoons soft brown sugar. Process for 20 seconds at a time, scraping down the side of the bowl each time, until the mixture forms a smooth paste. Add 2 tablespoons fish sauce and 3 tablespoons cold water and process until smooth. A little more water can be added if a thinner consistency is required. Refrigerate in an airtight container for up to 1 month.

Hot green mango sauce

MAKES APPROXIMATELY 185 ML (6 FL OZ/¾ CUP)

Combine 2 chopped garlic cloves, 3 chopped French shallots (eschalots), ¼ teaspoon freshly ground black pepper, 1 teaspoon dried shrimp and 1 teaspoon shrimp paste in a mortar and pestle or small food processor. Pound or process until finely chopped and then stir in 1 tablespoon soft brown sugar, ½ finely grated green mango and 2 tablespoons cold water. This sauce is best used within 12 hours.

Quick chilli sauce

MAKES APPROXIMATELY 125 ML (4 FL OZ/½ CUP)

Trim the stems from 6 large, fresh red chillies. Cut the chillies open (remove the seeds for a milder flavour) and soak for 15 minutes in hot water. Place in a food processor with 3 tablespoons white vinegar, 90 g (3¼ oz/ ⅓ cup) caster (superfine) sugar, 1 teaspoon salt and 4 chopped garlic cloves. Process until smooth. Transfer to a small pan and cook for 15 minutes over medium heat, stirring frequently, until the sauce has thickened. Allow to cool and then stir in 2 teaspoons fish sauce. Hint: To make sweet chilli sauce, increase the sugar to 230 g (8½ oz/1 cup).

Sour sauce

MAKES APPROXIMATELY 125 ML (4 FL OZ/½ CUP)

In a bowl, combine 3 tablespoons fish sauce, 2 tablespoons white vinegar and 2 tablespoons lime juice. Chopped fresh coriander (cilantro) leaves can be added if you are serving a Thai dish.

Tamarind and chilli sauce

MAKES APPROXIMATELY 125 ML (4 FL OZ/½ CUP)

Heat 1 tablespoon oil in a wok, add 4 finely chopped French shallots (eschalots) and 2 chopped garlic cloves and stir for 2 minutes over low heat. Add 1–2 teaspoons chopped fresh red chillies and stir-fry for 30 seconds. Add 3 tablespoons tamarind purée and 1 tablespoon soft brown sugar. Bring to the boil, stirring, and then reduce the heat and simmer for 5 minutes. Allow to cool before serving. Can be seasoned with a little lime juice.

Flavoured cooking oils

Coriander oil

MAKES 375 ML (13 FL OZ/1½ CUPS)

Blanch the leaves, stems and roots of 180 g (6 oz/2 bunches) coriander (cilantro) in simmering water for 10 seconds. Remove and plunge into iced water. Drain well and pat dry with paper towels. Chop the coriander roughly, then process with 375 ml (13 fl oz/1½ cups) oil in a food processor. Seal in a sterilised glass jar and refrigerate overnight. Strain through a fine sieve and discard any solids. Store in a sterilised glass jar in the fridge for up to 2 weeks.

Garlic oil

MAKES 375 ML (13 FL OZ/1½ CUPS)

Peel one garlic bulb, place in a bowl and cover with white vinegar or lemon juice for 24 hours. Drain, discard the vinegar and dry the garlic on paper towels. Place the garlic in a wok with 375 ml (13 fl oz/1½ cups) oil, heat to 105°C (220°F) and cook for 12 minutes, or until the garlic begins to turn golden. Pour into a sterilised glass jar, seal, cool and refrigerate overnight. Strain, discard the garlic and store the oil in a sterilised glass jar in the fridge for up to 6 weeks.

Ginger oil

MAKES 375 ML (13 FL OZ/1½ CUPS)

Heat 375 ml (13 fl oz/1½ cups) oil and 400 g (14 oz) finely sliced fresh ginger in a wok to 105°C (220°F) and cook for 45 minutes, or until the ginger just starts to turn golden. Strain the oil and discard the ginger. Pour the oil into a sterilised glass jar, seal, cool and store in the fridge for up to 6 months.

Lime and lemongrass oil

MAKES 375 ML (13 FL OZ/1½ CUPS)

Finely chop the white part of 2 lemongrass stems (peel off the tough outer layer and chop away the tough, green end). Pour 375 ml (13 fl oz/1½ cups) oil into a wok and add the lemongrass and the sliced zest of 4 limes. Heat to 105°C (220°F) and cook for 5 minutes, then add 4 shredded makrut (kaffir lime) leaves. Remove from the heat. Pour into a sterilised glass jar, seal, cool and refrigerate for 2 days, then strain, discarding the solids. Store in a sterilised glass jar in the fridge for up to 6 months.

Sesame and chilli oil

MAKES 375 ML (13 FL OZ/1½ CUPS)

Heat 300 ml (10½ fl oz) oil and 3 tablespoons chilli flakes in a wok to 105°C (220°F) and cook for 8 minutes. Remove from the heat and add 80 ml (2½ fl oz/⅓ cup) sesame oil. Strain and discard the chillies. Pour into a sterilised glass jar, seal, cool and store in the fridge for up to 6 months.

Star anise and orange oil

MAKES 375 ML (13 FL OZ/1½ CUPS)

Heat 300 ml (10½ fl oz) oil with 80 ml (2½ fl oz/⅓ cup) good-quality peanut oil, 4 star anise and the zest of 4 large oranges in a wok to 105°C (220°F) and cook for 5 minutes. Pour into a sterilised glass jar, seal, cool and refrigerate for 2 days to infuse. Strain and discard the solids. Store in the fridge for up to 6 months.

Index

Index

A

Asian greens and mushrooms 228
Asian greens with teriyaki tofu
    dressing 210
Asian peppered beef 32
asparagus
    asparagus stir-fried with
        mustard 236
    chicken and asparagus 123
    chicken with beans and
        asparagus 141
    crab with asparagus and
        broccoli 187
    peppered lamb and asparagus 90

B

Balinese chilli squid 190
bean vermicelli and crabmeat 181
beans
    chicken with beans and
        asparagus 141
    green beans with shiitake
        mushrooms 222
    pork and green beans with
        ginger sauce 49
    pork with snake beans 68
    tamari almonds with spicy green
        beans 231
    Thai-spiced cauliflower and
        snake beans 225
    Vietnamese prawns with snake
        beans 192
    see also black beans
beef
    Asian peppered beef 32
    beef with bok choy 37
    beef with leeks and snow peas 39
    beef with oyster sauce 16
    beef with shiitake mushrooms 21
    beef with spinach 24
    beef, vermicelli and Thai basil
        salad 31
    black bean beef with noodles 13
    chilli beef with Chinese
        spinach 26
    Chinese beef and snow peas 17
    coriander beef 25
    fresh rice noodles with beef 28
    Mandarin beef 23
    marinated lemongrass beef 12
    mee goreng 18
    nasi goreng 34

quick beef and noodle salad 15
Thai beef salad 20
Thai braised beef with spinach
    and leeks 29
Thai green curry 36
Thai red curry 33
warm citrus beef salad 10
black beans
    black bean beef with noodles 13
    black bean and chilli mussels 171
    black bean pork with bok choy 52
    black bean scallops in ginger
        chilli oil 169
    noodles with chicken and black
        beans 126
    scallops with black bean
        sauce 179
    squid in black bean and chilli
        sauce 158
black fungus
    black fungus with prawns 185
    ginger chicken with black
        fungus 127
bok choy
    beef with bok choy 37
    black bean pork with bok
        choy 52
    duck, orange and bok choy 98
    rice sticks with chicken and
        greens 120
    swordfish with bok choy 177
    tofu with bok choy 215
broccoli
    Chinese pork with broccoli 45
    crab with asparagus and
        broccoli 187
    rice sticks with chicken and
        greens 120
    butter chicken 107

C

caramel coriander chicken 133
cashew nuts
    chilli lamb and cashews 91
    citrus chilli pork with cashew
        nuts 60
    pork with pumpkin and cashew
        nuts 44
    Vietnamese chicken with
        pineapple and cashews 99
    cauliflower and snake beans,
        Thai-spiced 225
Chiang Mai noodles 69

chicken
    butter chicken 107
    caramel coriander chicken 133
    chicken and asparagus 123
    chicken with beans and asparagus
        141
    chicken chow mein 104
    chicken nasi goreng 117
    chicken with oyster sauce and
        basil 106
    chicken san choy bau 135
    chicken with snow pea
        sprouts 143
    chicken with snow peas 111
    chicken with soy and hokkien
        noodles 110
    chicken with walnuts and straw
        mushrooms 125
    chilli-crusted chicken
        noodles 146
    country chicken kapitan 128
    curried chicken noodles 142
    ginger chicken with black fungus
        127
    Goan-style chicken with sultanas
        and almonds 96
    honey chicken 122
    lemon chicken 138
    Middle Eastern chicken 103
    nasi goreng chicken 117
    nonya lime chicken 115
    noodles with chicken and black
        beans 126
    orange chilli chicken in lettuce
        cups 144
    peppered chicken 134
    quick Thai chicken 147
    rice sticks with chicken and
        greens 120
    sesame chicken and leek 118
    sichuan pepper chicken 109
    soy chicken and crisp noodles 136
    sweet chilli chicken 139
    tangy orange and ginger
        chicken 112
    Thai chicken and basil 130
    Thai red curry noodles and
        chicken 119
    Vietnamese chicken with
        pineapple and cashews 99
    Vietnamese chicken salad 114
    warm curried chicken salad 101
    wok-fried chicken and
        lemongrass 131

chilli
    Balinese chilli squid 190
    black bean and chilli mussels 171
    black bean scallops in ginger
        chilli oil 169
    chilli beef with Chinese
        spinach 26
    chilli lamb and cashews 91
    chilli noodles and nuts 234
    chilli squid with sugar snap
        peas 165
    chilli tempeh 202
    chilli-crusted chicken
        noodles 146
    citrus chilli pork with cashew
        nuts 60
    fish cutlets in spicy red
        sauce 157
    fried clams in roasted chilli paste
        168
    marinated chilli squid 193
    orange chilli chicken in lettuce
        cups 144
    quick chilli sauce 248
    seafood with chilli plum
        sauce 184
    spicy chilli prawns 152
    squid in black bean and chilli
        sauce 158
    sweet chilli chicken 139
    sweet chilli squid 196
Chinese beef and snow peas 17
Chinese pork with broccoli 45
Chinese pork sausages 71
Chinese tofu 206
citrus
    citrus chilli pork with cashew
        nuts 60
    warm citrus beef salad 10
    see also lemon; lime; orange
clams, fried, in roasted chilli
    paste 168
coconut
    fish fillets in coconut milk 166
    peppered coconut pork fillet 58
    vegetables stir-fried in coconut
        milk 227
coriander beef 25
coriander oil 249
coriander pork with fresh
    pineapple 73
corn
    fried tofu, choy sum and baby
        corn in oyster sauce 211

Thai red pork curry with corn and peas 72

crab
bean vermicelli and crabmeat 181
crab with asparagus and broccoli 187

curry
curried chicken noodles 142
curried lobster with capsicum 155
curried sweet potato 233
duck and pineapple curry 102
Malay fish curry 153
pork ball curry with egg noodles 64
red vegetable curry 226
Thai green curry 36
Thai red curry 33
Thai red curry noodles and chicken 119
Thai red pork curry with corn and peas 72
Thai red pork and pumpkin curry 53
Thai wok-curried vegetables 242
warm curried chicken salad 101

curry pastes 246–47

D

dip, pork and peanut 77
dressings
lemon 101
mint 80
duck
duck, orange and bok choy 98
duck and pineapple curry 102

E

eggplant
eggplant with hot bean sauce 235
spicy lamb and eggplant 88
eggs
prawn omelette 156
savoury rice and eggs 74

F

fish
fish cutlets in spicy red sauce 157
fish fillets in coconut milk 166
fish with ginger 160
Malay fish curry 153
scallops and fish in ginger and lime 164

swordfish with bok choy 177
see also seafood

G

garlic
garlic and ginger prawns 172
garlic lamb with wilted mushrooms and noodles 85
ginger garlic prawn salad 195
garlic oil 249
ginger
baby octopus with ginger and lime 174
black bean scallops in ginger chilli oil 169
fish with ginger 160
garlic and ginger prawns 172
ginger chicken with black fungus 127
ginger garlic prawn salad 195
ginger oil 249
pork and green beans with ginger sauce 49
scallops and fish in ginger and lime 164
tangy orange and ginger chicken 112
udon noodles with ginger pork and pickles 50
Goan-style chicken with sultanas and almonds 96
green curry paste 246
green mango sauce, hot 248

H

hokkien noodles
chicken with soy and hokkien noodles 110
chilli-crusted chicken noodles 146
chilli noodles and nuts 234
deep-fried noodles with hokkien noodles 203
fried Korean noodles with prawns 173
mee goreng 18
mushroom noodles 243
noodles with chicken and black beans 126
quick beef and noodle salad 15
sichuan prawns with hokkien noodles 163
sweet chilli chicken 139
honey chicken 122
honey-braised vegetables with bean curd 205
hot green mango sauce 248

I

Indian lamb and spinach 87

K

kecap manis
beef with leeks and snow peas 39
chicken nasi goreng 117
chilli tempeh 202
Chinese pork with broccoli 45
fried rice noodles 71
Malay fish curry 153
nasi goreng 34
tofu and peanut noodles 207
tofu with bok choy 215
udon noodles wth vegetables 238

L

lamb
chilli lamb and cashews 91
garlic lamb with wilted mushrooms and noodles 85
Indian lamb and spinach 87
lamb with mixed greens 93
Mongolian lamb 82
peppered lamb and asparagus 90
satay lamb 83
spicy lamb and eggplant 88
sweet mustard lamb 86
warm lamb salad 80
larb (spicy Thai pork salad) 57
leeks
beef with leeks and snow peas 39
sesame chicken and leek 118
Thai braised beef with spinach and leeks 29
lemon chicken 138
lemon dressing 101
lemon sauce 138
lemongrass
lemongrass prawns 197
marinated lemongrass beef 12
mussels with lemongrass, basil and wine 188
wok-fried chicken and lemongrass 131
lime
baby octopus with ginger and lime 174
nonya lime chicken 115
prawn salad with makrut 161
scallops and fish in ginger and lime 164

lime and lemongrass oil 249
lobster, curried, with capsicum 155
lup chiang 71

M

ma por tofu 65
Malay fish curry 153
Mandarin beef 23
marinated lemongrass beef 12
mee goreng 18
Middle Eastern chicken 103
mint dressing 80
Mongolian lamb 82
Musaman curry paste 246
mushrooms
Asian greens and mushrooms 228
beef with shiitake mushrooms 21
black fungus with prawns 185
chicken with walnuts and straw mushrooms 125
fried noodles with mushrooms and barbecued pork 61
garlic lamb with wilted mushrooms and noodles 85
ginger chicken with black fungus 127
green beans with shiitake mushrooms 222
mushroom noodles 243
mushrooms with Thai basil 223
mussels
black bean and chilli mussels 171
mussels with lemongrass, basil and wine 188
mustard
asparagus stir-fried with mustard 236
sweet mustard lamb 86

N

nam prik
basic sauce (nam prik) 248
Chiang Mai noodles 69
nasi goreng
beef 34
chicken 117
nonya lime chicken 115
noodles
bean vermicelli and crabmeat 181
black bean beef with noodles 13
Chiang Mai noodles 69

chicken with soy and hokkien
noodles 110
chilli noodles and nuts 234
chilli-crusted chicken noodles
146
curried chicken noodles 142
deep-fried tofu with hokkien
noodles 203
fresh rice noodles with beef 28
fried Korean noodles with
prawns 173
fried noodles with mushrooms
and barbecued pork 61
fried rice noodles 71
garlic lamb with wilted
mushrooms and noodles 85
mushroom noodles 243
noodles with chicken and black
beans 126
pork ball curry with egg
noodles 64
potato noodles with
vegetables 220
quick beef and noodle salad 15
rice sticks with chicken and
greens 120
sichuan prawns with hokkien
noodles 163
soy chicken and crisp noodles
136
sweet and sour noodles 241
Thai crispy fried noodles 55
Thai noodles with bean
curd 216
Thai red curry noodles and
chicken 119
tofu and peanut noodles 207
udon noodles with vegetables
238
vegetarian phad thai 208

O

octopus, baby, with ginger and
lime 174
oils, flavoured 249
orange
duck, orange and bok choy 98
orange chilli chicken in lettuce
cups 144
tangy orange and ginger
chicken 112

P

Panang curry paste 247

pepper
Asian peppered beef 32
peppered chicken 134
peppered coconut pork fillet 58
peppered lamb and asparagus
90
sichuan pepper chicken 109
phad thai 66
vegetarian 208
pineapple
coriander pork with fresh
pineapple 73
duck and pineapple curry 102
Vietnamese chicken with
pineapple and cashews 99
pork
black bean pork with bok choy
52
Chiang Mai noodles 69
Chinese pork with broccoli 45
citrus chilli pork with cashew
nuts 60
coriander pork with fresh
pineapple 73
fried noodles with mushrooms
and barbecued pork 61
fried rice with coriander and
basil 76
fried rice noodles 71
larb (spicy Thai pork salad) 57
ma por tofu 65
peppered coconut pork fillet 58
phad thai 66
pork ball curry with egg
noodles 64
pork and green beans with
ginger sauce 49
pork and peanut dip 77
pork with pumpkin and cashew
nuts 44
pork with snake beans 68
san choy bau 63
savoury rice and eggs 74
sesame pork 48
sichuan pork with capsicum 47
spicy sausage stir-fry 56
sweet and sour pork 42
Thai crispy fried noodles 55
Thai red pork curry with corn
and peas 72
Thai red pork and pumpkin
curry 53
udon noodles with ginger pork
and pickles 50
potato noodles with vegetables
220

prawns
black fungus with prawns 185
fried Korean noodles with
prawns 173
garlic and ginger prawns 172
ginger garlic prawn salad 195
lemongrass prawns 197
phad thai 66
prawn fried rice 180
prawn omelette 156
prawn salad with makrut 161
prawns and scallops with Thai
spices 189
san choy bau 63
sichuan prawns with hokkien
noodles 163
spicy chilli prawns 152
Vietnamese prawns with snake
beans 192
warm prawn and scallop
salad 182
pumpkin
pork with pumpkin and cashew
nuts 44
Thai red pork and pumpkin
curry 53

R

red curry paste 247
red vegetable curry 226
rice
fried rice with coriander and
basil 76
prawn fried rice 180
savoury rice and eggs 74
rice noodles, fresh, with beef 28
rice sticks with chicken and greens
120
rice wine vinegar 49

S

salt-and-pepper squid 150
san choy bau
chicken 135
pork 63
satay lamb 83
sauces, serving
basic sauce (nam prik) 248
cooked hot chilli sauce 248
hot green mango sauce 248
lemon sauce 138
quick chilli sauce 248
sour sauce 248
tamarind and chilli sauce 248

sausage stir-fry, spicy 56
savoury rice and eggs 74
scallops
black bean scallops in ginger
chilli oil 169
prawns and scallops with Thai
spices 189
scallops with black bean
sauce 179
scallops and fish in ginger and
lime 164
warm prawn and scallop
salad 182
seafood
baby octopus with ginger and
lime 174
Balinese chilli squid 190
bean vermicelli and crabmeat
181
black bean and chilli mussels
171
black bean scallops in ginger
chilli oil 169
black fungus with prawns 185
chilli squid with sugar snap peas
165
crab with asparagus and
broccoli 187
curried lobster with capsicum
155
fish cutlets in spicy red sauce 157
fish fillets in coconut milk 166
fish with ginger 160
fried clams in roasted chilli
paste 168
fried Korean noodles with
prawns 173
garlic and ginger prawns 172
ginger garlic prawn salad 195
lemongrass prawns 197
Malay fish curry 153
marinated chilli squid 193
mussels with lemongrass, basil
and wine 188
prawn fried rice 180
prawn omelette 156
prawn salad with makrut 161
prawns and scallops with Thai
spices 189
salt-and-pepper squid 150
scallops with black bean
sauce 179
scallops and fish in ginger and
lime 164
seafood with chilli plum
sauce 184

seafood with mirin 176
sichuan prawns with hokkien
    noodles 163
spicy chilli prawns 152
squid in black bean and chilli
    sauce 158
sweet chilli squid 196
swordfish with bok choy 177
Vietnamese prawns with snake
    beans 192
warm prawn and scallop
    salad 182
sesame chicken and leek 118
sesame and chilli oil 249
sesame pork 48
sichuan pepper chicken 109
sichuan pork with capsicum 47
sichuan prawns with hokkien
    noodles 163
sour sauce 248
soy chicken and crisp noodles 136
spicy chilli prawns 152
spicy lamb and eggplant 88
spicy sausage stir-fry 56
spicy Thai pork salad 57
spinach
    beef with spinach 24
    chilli beef with Chinese
        spinach 26
    Indian lamb and spinach 87
    seafood with chilli plum
        sauce 184
    Thai braised beef with spinach
        and leeks 29
squid
    Balinese chilli squid 190
    chilli squid with sugar snap
        peas 165
    marinated chilli squid 193
    salt-and-pepper squid 150
    squid in black bean and chilli
        sauce 158
    sweet chilli squid 196
star anise and orange oil 249
sweet chilli chicken 139
sweet chilli squid 196
sweet mustard lamb 86
sweet potato, curried 233
sweet and sour noodles 241
sweet and sour pork 42
swordfish with bok choy 177

T

tamari almonds with spicy green
    beans 231

tamarind and chilli sauce 248
tempeh
    chilli tempeh 202
    tempeh with Chinese greens 214
Thai beef salad 20
Thai braised beef with spinach
    and leeks 29
Thai chicken, quick 147
Thai chicken and basil 130
Thai crispy fried noodles 55
Thai green curry 36
Thai noodles with bean curd 216
Thai red curry 33
Thai red curry noodles and
    chicken 119
Thai red pork curry with corn and
    peas 72
Thai red pork and pumpkin
    curry 53
Thai wok-curried vegetables 242
Thai-spiced cauliflower and snake
    beans 225
tofu
    Asian greens with teriyaki tofu
        dressing 210
    Chinese tofu 206
    crisp tofu in hot bean sauce 200
    deep-fried tofu with hokkien
        noodles 203
    fried tofu, choy sum and baby
        corn in oyster sauce 211
    honey-braised vegetables with
        bean curd 205
    ma por tofu 65
    Thai noodles with bean curd
        216
    tofu with bok choy 215
    tofu and peanut noodles 207
    tofu with shoshoyu and mirin 213
    vegetarian phad thai 208

U

udon noodles
    with ginger pork and pickles 50
    with vegetables 238

V

vegetables
    Asian greens and mushrooms
        228
    Asian greens with teriyaki tofu
        dressing 210
    asparagus stir-fried with
        mustard 236

chilli noodles and nuts 234
curried sweet potato 233
eggplant with hot bean sauce 235
fragrant greens 230
green beans with shiitake
    mushrooms 222
honey-braised vegetables with
    bean curd 205
mushroom noodles 243
mushrooms with Thai basil 223
potato noodles with vegetables
    220
red vegetable curry 226
sweet and sour noodles 241
tamari almonds with spicy green
    beans 231
tempeh with Chinese greens 214
Thai wok-curried vegetables 242
Thai-spiced cauliflower and
    snake beans 225
udon noodles with vegetables
    238
vegetables with honey and soy
    239
vegetables stir-fried in coconut
    milk 227
vegetarian phad thai 208
Vietnamese chicken with
    pineapple and cashews 99
Vietnamese chicken salad 114
Vietnamese prawns with snake
    beans 192

Published in 2008 by Murdoch Books Pty Limited.

Murdoch Books Australia
Pier 8/9, 23 Hickson Road
Millers Point NSW 2000
Phone: + 61 (0) 2 8220 2000
Fax: + 61 (0) 2 8220 2558
www.murdochbooks.com.au

Murdoch Books UK Limited
Erico House, 6th Floor
93–99 Upper Richmond Road
Putney, London SW15 2TG
Phone: + 44 (0) 20 8785 5995
Fax: + 44 (0) 20 8785 5985
www.murdochbooks.co.uk

Chief Executive: Juliet Rogers
Publishing Director: Kay Scarlett

Project manager and editor: Paul O'Beirne
Design concept: Heather Menzies
Design: Heather Menzies and Jacqueline Richards
Photographer: Natasha Milne
Stylist: Vicki Liley
Food preparation: Christopher Tate, Samantha Joel and Wendy Quisumbing
Introduction text: Leanne Kitchen
Production: Monique Layt

©Text, design and illustrations Murdoch Books Pty Limited 2008. All rights reserved.
No part of this publication may be reproduced, stored in a retrieval system or transmitted in any form or by any means,
electronic, mechanical, photocopying, recording or otherwise without the prior written permission of the publisher.

National Library of Australia Cataloguing-in-Publication Data
Homestyle Stir-fry. Includes index.
ISBN 978 1 74196 168 3 (pbk.).
1. Stir-frying cookery. I. Title. 641.774

A catalogue record for this book is available from the British Library.

Colour separation by Splitting Image in Clayton, Victoria, Australia.
Printed by i-Book Printing Ltd. in 2008. PRINTED IN CHINA.

IMPORTANT: Those who might be at risk from the effects of salmonella poisoning
(the elderly, pregnant women, young children and those suffering from immune deficiency diseases)
should consult their doctor with any concerns about eating raw eggs.

CONVERSION GUIDE: You may find cooking times vary depending on the oven
you are using. For fan-forced ovens, as a general rule, set the oven temperature to
20°C (35°F) lower than indicated in the recipe.